I open my eyes, feeli

to realize that I'm no

hotel room in Japan. I think I slept some, but not much.

The clock on the nightstand reads "02:05."

Adam is climbing into his bed. "Sorry, I didn't mean to wake you," he whispers. "Go back to sleep."

For some reason that I don't completely understand, I climb out of my bed, lift the covers on Adam's bed, and slip under them with him. I've only been in bed with Adam once before, on the night my dad died. I needed someone next to me that night. We didn't cuddle. We didn't even touch each other. We slept in his bed with a pillow between us. But it was comforting in exactly the way I needed to be comforted. Now, I don't *need* to be next to Adam, I *want* to be.

"Is something wrong?" Adam asks me.

"No, nothing's wrong," I say. And then I notice, "Hey, you're wearing the Japanese pajamas."

"You seemed so excited about them. I didn't want to let you down."

The way he says that makes it clear he's joking, but his words resonate with me. I've been let down many times in my life. By people I loved. People I trusted. But Adam has never, ever let me down.

As I stare into his eyes, I feel something stir inside me. Something I didn't think I'd ever feel again. A longing. I wrap my arms around Adam, and he pulls our bodies together, holding onto me so tightly that I feel his warmth through the two thin silky layers that separate us.

"Can I sleep here tonight?" I whisper.

He swallows. "Of course."

Praise for
LOST IN TOKYO

"Full of heartbreak, loss and finding yourself while falling in love with your best friend. I would absolutely recommend this book and I have to several people already."
– Amy, Goodreads

"Beautifully written ... emotional adventure. Quite a few scenes brought out the goosebumps." – Denise, Goodreads

"Japan as a backdrop was such a unique story setting. It was both peaceful and exciting at the same time."
– Amanda, Goodreads

"I absolutely loved this book! I couldn't put it down. The relationship between Erin and Adam was amazingly sensual and slow building. It kept the pages turning like crazy. And the way the plot kept unfolding, I never knew what was going to happen next. Lynne's use of imagery was fantastic, the characters were always the main focus, you felt like you were right there with them." – Amanda, Goodreads

"I did one of those 'start from the beginning' when I finished it - I wasn't ready to leave the world that Lynne had created!" – Janet, Goodreads

LOST IN TOKYO

J.W. LYNNE

This book is a work of fiction. Names, places, organizations, programs, businesses, incidents, etc. either are products of the author's imagination or are used fictitiously. All characters appearing in this work are fictitious. Any resemblance to actual persons, living or dead, is entirely coincidental.

ISBN 978-1500467814

To Peter, who traveled with me to Japan

* * * *

LOST IN TOKYO

Chapter One

My brain feels cloudy. I can't wait to slip into bed. But my bed is thousands of miles from here. And the bed where I'm supposed to spend tonight—in a hotel somewhere in a place called Shinjuku—feels like it's a million miles away.

Adam and I enter a cavernous room filled with zigzagging queues of bleary-eyed travelers. We join the line labeled "Foreigners" and pull out our passports. I open mine to my photo. Adam took that photo. It's one of the few that I've let anyone take of me over the past year, and it might be the only one taken in the past year where I'm genuinely smiling.

My name is printed out next to my photo in all capital letters: "ERIN BEATRICE WINTERS." My middle name is my mom's first name. I haven't seen my mom in almost fifteen years, but I have wonderful memories of the four years that we had together. I remember how we spent a steamy summer morning dancing in the sprinklers on our front lawn. And how we passed an afternoon sampling ice cream from every vendor we could find in Central Park. And how she taught me to dive under the waves at Jones Beach. But those memories are overshadowed by the one memory I wish I could forget. The memory of sitting in my mom's favorite chair, cuddling the worn purple corduroy blanket that my mom and I snuggled under when she read fairy tales to me. It was late at night and I couldn't fall asleep. I remember asking my father when Mommy was coming home to kiss me goodnight. His response tore a hole in my soul that I've never been able to fill: "She's not."

I slide my customs declaration form into my passport and take out my notes for the final leg of tonight's journey. There is a series of trains that connect Haneda Airport—where we are now—to Shinjuku—where we will spend our first few nights in Japan. The trains stop running from the airport just after midnight. And it's well past 11 PM. If we miss the last train of the night, our only option to get to Shinjuku is a long, expensive cab ride that I really can't afford. I've already budgeted nearly every last dollar of my savings to take this trip. Adam offered to pay for the cab ride, but I can't let him do that.

By the time I step up to an official-looking man at a

booth, there are six minutes until the final train of the night departs. The man scrutinizes my paperwork and then assesses me up and down with serious eyes. I swallow hard and try to keep my body relaxed. I don't like it when men look at me. I feel like they see me naked.

The man stamps my paperwork and passport and I move along. I breathe a quiet sigh of relief when Adam joins me, then I check my watch. "Three minutes!"

We rush forward.

"*Sumimasen*," I say to the first woman I see. I point to the place on my notes where I've written the name of the train that we need to take, hoping she'll offer directions.

She points across the way and says something in Japanese that I don't understand.

"*Arigato*," I thank her.

And then Adam and I run, dragging our suitcases behind us. We stop at a row of glowing screens near a set of turnstiles. It must be the place to purchase train tickets, but all of the writing on the screens is in Japanese. I stare at a screen, my heart beating fast. We don't have time to waste.

A woman wearing a uniform approaches us and says something in Japanese, possibly asking us if we need assistance.

"Shinjuku?" I try in response.

She pushes a few buttons on the screen in front of us and then asks, "Two?"

"*Hai*," Adam says.

He slides some yen into the machine, and it spits out a few coins and two tiny tickets, much smaller than any U.S. train tickets I've ever seen.

"*Arigato*," I say to the woman.

Adam and I insert our tickets into the adjacent turnstiles and then race through clean, empty, echoing passageways. We arrive at the track just in time to meet a sleek train, its doors still open.

As we settle into some seats, I exhale but don't relax.

We still need to get to our hotel in Shinjuku.

* * *

When the train stops in Shinagawa, we transfer to a train that will take us to Shinjuku after a brief stop in Osaki. The Shinagawa train has a surprising number of people on it, considering that it's after midnight. All of the other passengers are wearing suits or business attire. I look at Adam's tousled mop of blond hair and his green college hoodie that brings out the green in his eyes. I appear equally out of place in my rumpled pullover and sweatpants with my wavy, sandy-brown hair and pale skin. We are the only tourists in a sea of locals.

My tired eyes stare at Adam's hoodie; he was wearing it when we met, on the first day of college orientation, almost a year ago. That day didn't start out well. I was still living at my dad's house on Long Island—I hadn't moved into the dorms yet—and so I had to take a train and a subway to get to my school in New York City. My dad was planning to drive me to the train station that morning, but something came up at his work and he couldn't take me.

By the time I got to campus, I'd missed the orientation breakfast, the welcome talk, and the tour. The last activity of the morning was underway: an icebreaking session. Everyone had already split up into small groups and, based on all the laughing and talking that I observed through the student lounge window, it was obvious that the ice was broken.

As I entered the room, wishing I were invisible, I accidentally banged my shoulder against the doorframe, and everyone looked up. And then I saw the one person I was hoping to never see again for the rest of my life: Barry.

Barry's gaze met mine and a deep chill—cold enough to practically stop my heart—shot through my chest. I searched his eyes for some sign of remorse over what he'd done to me just a few weeks earlier, but I saw none. Instead, his lips curled into a smug smile. I stood there in the doorway, mustering every shred of strength that I had to hold back my tears. And then I felt a hand on my arm. I jumped.

A guy with unruly blond hair was standing next to me. "I think you're in our group," he said.

"What?" I stepped away from him. I couldn't handle having people stand so close to me.

He looked at the nametag that I'd forgotten I was

wearing. "You're Erin Winters, right?"

I nodded.

"Yup, you're in our group," he said. "I'm Adam."

Adam led me to a group of seven other freshmen and introduced me to them. Then Tara—one of the three girls in our group—said, "The next question we're supposed to answer is, 'What qualities do you look for in a friend?'"

We went around the circle, everyone listing an attribute which Tara then wrote on a notepad propped on an easel: loyal, caring, fun to be around, trustworthy, shares common interests, adventurous, sense of humor ...

"Honest," Adam added and then it was my turn.

Doesn't hurt me. That's what I needed in a friend. Of course, I couldn't say that, so I mumbled, "Yeah. Honest." And the group moved on.

After the icebreaking session, it was time for lunch. I was famished, but I needed to go get my student ID. I stared at my orientation map, trying to figure out how to get to the Registrar's Office.

"Looking for lunch?" a voice asked me. It was Adam.

"I need to pick up my student ID first," I said. "I didn't get it this morning because I was late, and I missed the campus tour, and now I have to go to the Registrar's Office, but I don't see it on the map ..." I took an exhausted breath.

"I'll show you where it is if you want."

I eyed him suspiciously, wondering why he was being so helpful. "Don't you want to go to lunch with everyone else?"

"They've been feeding us all morning. Besides, I could use a break from all the forced socializing. It's overwhelming."

"You don't seem like the kind of person who gets overwhelmed by that stuff."

He shrugged. "Well, I am. What kind of person are you?"

I guess he caught me off-guard because I said, "A really-messed-up kind of person."

Adam's forehead creased. "Humor?"

"Honesty," I admitted.

He smiled the warmest smile I'd ever seen. "I like honesty."

"Me too." I felt myself relax. Adam made me feel like everything I was feeling ... everything I *was* ... was okay.

"Want me to give you that tour?" he asked.

I said yes.

I never imagined that, not even a year later, Adam and I would be touring *Japan*.

* * *

When the train stops in Osaki, the business people get off. Adam and I are now the only ones left on the train. I look at the advertisements lining the top of each wall of the train and hanging down from the center of the ceiling. They are more bold and colorful than ads back home.

I point to a poster with a cartoon picture of a frog-shaped boat sailing in a pink-and-purple lake. "What do you think that ad is for?" I ask Adam. Normally I would look to the words for clues, but of course all of the words on the poster are in Japanese. I feel a bit like a child. My nineteen years of life experience isn't offering the kind of help it should.

Before Adam can answer me, a grey-haired businessman boards the train, waving at us. He says something in Japanese.

"*Wakarimasen,*" Adam says, shaking his head with confusion.

The man tries again, speaking slowly, urgently. He points to the train full of passengers across the platform and moves his hand from us to it.

I point to my notes. "Shinjuku." I say to the man.

"Shinjuku," he repeats, gesturing to the adjacent train.

I look up and down the deserted train car that we occupy. "We can't be the only people heading to Shinjuku."

We follow the man into the other train. As we find some seats, the train that we just left behind starts moving back the way it came. Back toward the airport. I am about to thank the man for his help, but he is already absorbed with his phone.

Adam gives me a "that guy just saved us" look. I give him a "yes, he did" nod back. We don't speak. No one on the train is talking; everyone is either occupied with an electronic device of some sort or resting their eyes as the train zips toward Shinjuku—*I hope*.

Nighttime Japan blurs past the train windows. I try to decipher what's out there in the darkness. Towering, dimly-lit office buildings. Mom-and-pop shops lining sidewalks. Black, mysterious trees. A large sign made out of balloons?

When a computerized female voice announces that the next stop is Shinjuku, the grey-haired businessman looks up. Seeing us gather our belongings, he returns his attention to his phone. *He was looking out for us again.* I feel a flood of gratitude for this stranger. He knows we are lost. He could have ignored us, or worse, taken advantage of us, but he didn't. He helped us.

And then I realize—in this unfamiliar world, where we know no one and can't speak the language—just how vulnerable we are.

* * *

We exit the train station onto the streets of Shinjuku. This part of the city reminds me of an abandoned movie set. The traffic lights that alternate from green to yellow to red and the hundreds of glowing billboards make it appear to be a living, breathing city, yet there are no cars. No people. It's alive and yet devoid of life.

I pull out the hotel confirmation page with its tiny map, and Adam and I study it.

"I think the hotel is this way," I say, pointing to our

right.

We start walking.

Every street we cross is deserted. I feel like we're heading deeper and deeper into a post-apocalyptic world. In New York City, I felt this way only once: this past Christmas when I took a stroll early in the morning to try to forget the ache in my heart from having essentially become an orphan one week earlier—when my father died. I felt so completely alone then.

Now I'm not alone. Adam is by my side. And in this foreign world—with signs we can't read and storefronts similar to those in New York, but disconcertingly unfamiliar—Adam appears intrigued rather than apprehensive. He makes me feel like everything's going to be okay.

Suddenly, a Japanese man wearing a business suit with a loosened tie rounds a corner and comes toward us at a brisk pace. I hate to disturb him, but he might be our only option for directions.

"Let's ask him if he knows the way," I suggest to Adam.

"*Eigo o hanasemasu ka*?" Adam calls out.

The man stops and smiles at us. "Yes, I speak English."

"We're looking for this hotel." I thrust our hotel confirmation letter toward him and then wonder if maybe I shouldn't be so trusting.

"It isn't far, just a few blocks. I'll show you." He turns and starts walking back the way he came. "Where are the two of you from?"

"New York," Adam says.

The man nods. "I'm afraid I've never been to New York. I spent ten years in London and always meant to get over to the U.S., but I never did. Someday I will make it there. What brings you to Japan?"

I hesitate.

Adam answers, "My ex-girlfriend is from Japan. She used to show me photos and videos of places that seemed so different and fascinating that I wished I could step into them and explore." Adam and Natsumi met in ninth grade and dated all through high school. Then Natsumi went to college in Connecticut, and Adam went to college in New York. Practically every weekend, Adam would take the train up to see her, or she would come down to visit him. They broke up four months ago.

The man is looking at me. "And you?"

"I think my mom might have come here … when I was a little kid … Or at least she wanted to."

I don't tell him the rest of the story. I don't tell him that, just after my fourth birthday, my mom went away— telling my father that she was going to spend the weekend with her best friend—and she never came home.

It turned out that my mom hadn't made plans with her best friend for that weekend. My mom's best friend had no idea where my mom went, but her best guess was that she had decided to travel the world. Apparently, my mom had a restless soul.

I don't have a restless soul. I never really had any desire to travel. My mom is the sole reason I came to Japan. Years before she disappeared, my mom wrote up a Japan bucket list—a detailed list of the things she wanted to do in Japan. She gave a copy to her best friend, saying that they should go there together someday with their children. My mom vanished before that happened.

A year ago, my mom's best friend gave me a copy of the Japan bucket list. The moment I saw it, I knew I had to come here. I don't know whether my mom ever made it to Japan, but I know she wanted to. And my mom wanted *me* to go with her. That's why I'm here. My mom's bucket list is in my backpack. It's my itinerary for this trip. I'm determined to do everything on her list.

"There you are." The man points down a street. The illuminated sign for our hotel peeks out over the top of a neighboring restaurant.

Relief washes over me. *We made it.*

"*Arigato gozaimasu,*" I thank the man.

"Cheers," he says. And then he dashes off, leaving us alone to walk the final block to our hotel.

* * *

The air inside our hotel room smells like bleach and

honeysuckles; it's not unpleasant, but it's *different*. I make my way down an entry hallway so narrow that I have to carefully guide my suitcase so it doesn't scrape against the scarred walls.

The bedroom is about half the size of my dorm room. It's barely big enough to accommodate the two twin beds that take up almost all of its floor space. The beds are separated by a remarkably-skinny nightstand that's dwarfed by the normal-sized alarm clock on top of it. It is 1:08 AM.

I heave my suitcase and backpack onto the nearest bed. Adam drops his suitcase and backpack onto the other bed and collapses next to them. I can't imagine spending the next five nights cramped in this tiny room alone, much less with another person. Until now, I hadn't really considered how strange it will be to share a bedroom with Adam. Although we are best friends, we've never been roommates before. I wonder if it will be awkward.

"Do you want to take the first shower?" Adam asks me.

"Sure. Thanks," I say.

And then I notice neatly-folded, white, silk pajamas on my bed. There are some on Adam's bed too.

"Japanese pajamas!" I exclaim, lifting what turns out to be a long nightshirt. "We should wear these!"

"I think I'll wear shorts and a t-shirt," Adam says.

"Suit yourself." I unzip my suitcase, grab my toiletries, and head into the bathroom.

As I brush my teeth, I examine the toilet. It looks like any ordinary toilet back home, except that, on one side, it has an armrest-like thing with numerous buttons that are labeled in Japanese. There are symbols on the buttons also, but I don't know what they mean.

After I rinse the toothpaste from my mouth, I sit on the toilet. "Whoa!" The seat is warm! It's comforting in a weird way to sit on a warm toilet seat—unless it's still warm from the person before you, which I'm sure is not the case here. I push the first button: a big orange circle with a square inside. Nothing happens. And then my foggy mind realizes it's the stop button. *Good. If I push a button with an outcome I don't like, I can put an end to it quickly.* I push the next button: a blue person sitting on a blue stool. "Aaah!" Warm water tickles my bottom. *Strange.* I push the button with the square. The water flow instantly stops. The next button is a red person on a red stool. The red stool is angled slightly differently than the blue stool. "Eeee." I feel a little like I'm peeing in reverse. "Adam, you've gotta try this toilet," I call out. I'm sure it feels different from a guy's perspective, but it's probably still an interesting experience.

"Based on what I'm hearing, I look forward to it," he calls back.

I laugh, pee, wipe, and flush. Then I poke my head out of the bathroom. "Do you need to use the restroom before I get in the shower?"

Adam smiles sleepily at me. "No, I'm fine."

The shower is less complicated than the toilet. I get it going, strip off my clothes, and step inside. As the warm water washes over me, it takes with it the stress of the past twenty-four hours.

But it can't budge the anxiety over what is to come.

* * *

I open my eyes, feeling disoriented. It takes me a moment to realize that I'm not in my dorm room, but rather in a hotel room in Japan. I think I slept some, but not much.

The clock on the nightstand reads "02:05."

Adam is climbing into his bed. "Sorry, I didn't mean to wake you," he whispers. "Go back to sleep."

For some reason that I don't completely understand, I climb out of my bed, lift the covers on Adam's bed, and slip under them with him. I've only been in bed with Adam once before, on the night my dad died. I needed someone next to me that night. We didn't cuddle. We didn't even touch each other. We slept in his bed with a pillow between us. But it was comforting in exactly the way I needed to be comforted. Now, I don't *need* to be next to Adam, I *want* to be.

"Is something wrong?" Adam asks me.

"No, nothing's wrong," I say. And then I notice, "Hey, you're wearing the Japanese pajamas."

"You seemed so excited about them. I didn't want to

let you down."

The way he says that makes it clear he's joking, but his words resonate with me. I've been let down many times in my life. By people I loved. People I trusted. But Adam has never, ever let me down.

As I stare into his eyes, I feel something stir inside me. Something I didn't think I'd ever feel again. A longing. I wrap my arms around Adam, and he pulls our bodies together, holding onto me so tightly that I feel his warmth through the two thin silky layers that separate us.

"Can I sleep here tonight?" I whisper.

He swallows. "Of course."

Chapter Two

A heavy arm is draped across my chest. I open my eyes, expecting to see Adam, but I see … Barry. My pulse pounds in my ears, deafening me. I'm in Barry's messy, darkened apartment. My entire body is sore, and no doubt bruised. The taste of beer lingers in my mouth, but I am sober now.

"Look who's awake," Barry says. He gives a carefree smile and adds, "Last night was fun."

Fun? That word hits me like a punch in the gut. *It wasn't fun. You hurt me.*

"Take me home." I start to get up, but Barry grabs me by the ribs.

"Not yet," he says flatly.

And then I realize: *He's going to do it to me again.*

Barry climbs on top of me. I want to make him stop, but he's twice my size and solid muscle, and if I try to fight, he might kill me. Last night, when I shouted for help, he put a pillow over my face and beat me until I surrendered to him.

Tears well in my eyes. "Barry, no," I whisper.

He slams his fist into the center of my chest, painfully forcing the air from my lungs and sending a shock wave into my arms. "Shut up."

I feel my underwear slip down.

Barry was my best friend all through elementary school. Our friendship was innocent. We took nature walks at the park and had picnics in his backyard and went for rides on his father's sailboat. In junior high school, we grew apart, but last night, the night of our senior prom, we started talking again. His date, just one of the many girls he'd dated during our four years at high school, had gotten sick at the last minute and mine, a friend, couldn't attend due to a family emergency.

Barry and I spent the whole evening together, and then he invited me to an afterparty that he and his friends were throwing on the roof of the New York City apartment building they'd just moved into. We were both going to go to the same college, so the reconnection made sense. But Barry didn't want me to be his friend. He wanted me in a different way. He tried to seduce me. When that didn't work, he took what he wanted. Violently.

Barry's body jams into me, hard and fast, stabbing my insides like a knife cutting all the way into my soul. Over and over again. I feel like it will never stop.

I need to fight him, even if he kills me.

If he kills me, he can't hurt me anymore.

I take every ounce of strength I have left, and shove him away.

"Hey!" Adam says.

My eyes snap open. I'm back in the hotel room in Shinjuku ... where I was all along.

"You okay?" Adam asks me.

I force myself to slow my rapid breathing. "I had a nightmare." *Is it a nightmare if it really happened? Or a memory?*

"About what?"

"Barry," I admit.

Adam rolls onto his side, facing me. "I thought you didn't have those nightmares anymore."

"I haven't had them in a while." After Barry, I had nightmares nearly every night, but once I told Adam about what Barry did to me, they stopped for good, or so I'd thought. Adam and I didn't do anything last night other than sleep in each other's arms. Even though friends don't normally do something as intimate as that, it shouldn't change anything. But it has. "I'm fine now," I say.

The concern doesn't fade from Adam's eyes. "We should probably get something to eat. Are you hungry?"

"I guess." I don't feel hungry, but I definitely should eat.

Adam climbs out of bed and heads to the bathroom.

I smooth my wild hair as best I can, and then I open the curtains covering the opaque window. I remember noticing that the window was opaque last night, but it didn't register as being strange until now. I release the safety latch, open the window as far as it will go, and peek through the six-inch gap. Tokyo looks … wet.

"It's raining," I tell Adam as he comes back into the room.

"Oh, okay," he says quietly.

I can tell that something's bothering him. Is it my nightmare? Or our night together? Or something else? I don't know if I'm ready for the answer.

I kneel next to the suitcase that I crammed under the desk last night—because that was the only place in this room where it fit—and pull out some quick-dry clothes. I decide to dress in layers, because I'm not sure what the day will bring.

But with the return of my nightmares about Barry, and my night spent cuddling with Adam, and the fact that these next few days may be the only chance I will ever have of finding my mother, the weather is the least of my worries.

* * *

The streets of Shinjuku are soaked, but it's no longer raining when we step onto the sidewalk in front of our hotel. Unlike last night, the city is bustling with people who move as if they are on an urgent mission. All of them wear dark slacks or suits with white shirts. I assume they're heading to work.

Restaurant windows along the busy streets display photos of chopped meat and fish. I read in my guidebooks that breakfast in Japan is traditionally just another meal. Cereal, toast, bagels, eggs, and muffins aren't usually on the menu. Even if I wasn't a vegetarian, I'm not sure I could handle meat or fish right now; my stomach feels queasy.

"Let's try in here," Adam says, gesturing to a store that looks like a 7-Eleven.

The sign above the window says, in English, "Family Mart."

As we step inside, the woman at the register shouts at us, without looking up from her work.

"Why did she yell at us?" Adam whispers to me.

"I'm pretty sure she said, '*Irasshaimase*,'" I say, "It's a greeting, like 'Welcome.'"

"Should we say something back?" Adam asks me.

A man wearing a business suit, carrying a long umbrella as if it's a walking stick, enters the store.

"*Irasshaimase!*" the store clerk shouts out.

The man doesn't respond at all.

I shrug. "Apparently not."

Adam and I turn our focus to the task at hand: trying to find something for breakfast. I spot a display of pastries that are individually wrapped in clear plastic. I choose a plain-looking one.

I find Adam in the refrigerated section, holding two packages of sushi.

I smile. "Sushi for breakfast?"

"Why not?"

"They have the kind you like," Adam says, pointing to a stack of packages of inari sushi—plain rice balls wrapped in sweet tofu skin.

I grab one of the packages.

On the way to the register, we pick up some fruit and I take a small box of candy that has the word "Chocolate," in English, on it.

I place my breakfast items on the counter by the register, and the woman rings them up. She points to the total amount on the cash register screen. I try to hand her a 1,000-yen note, but she gestures to a blue plastic tray near the register. When I put the bill in the tray, she quickly takes it and replaces it with my change.

"*Arigato gozaimasu,*" she says.

"*Arigato,*" I say, collecting my change and stuffing it into my wallet.

The woman rings up Adam's sushi and banana, he pays for them, and we walk out the door, joining the tide of business people streaming along the sidewalk.

"Where do you want to eat this stuff?" Adam asks me.

"Do you think we could find someplace peaceful?"

"We could try."

Adam and I sit on a bench in a tiny park tucked among gleaming skyscrapers, chatting the same easy way we usually do. I wonder if he has already forgotten our night together. Maybe I should too.

The air here has the pleasant smell of wet dirt. Directly ahead of us is a two-story, log-cabin-style playground fort topped with a lookout tower. On the weekends, every kid in the neighborhood must come play here, but now, on a weekday morning, the fort is unoccupied.

Adam follows my gaze. "You know you want to check that thing out," he prods.

"We're way too old," I say, eying the fort wistfully.

"There's no one here but us," Adam counters.

"Okay, why not?"

I drop the remnants of my breakfast into a trashcan and approach the fort. Sensing that Adam isn't with me, I glance back. Adam flashes a mischievous grin, then hops off the bench and barrels past me. I race after him.

He arrives at the fort first and bounds up a chain ladder to the second level. I climb the wooden ladder next to him. At the landing, Adam scrambles to his feet and disappears up some stairs. I rush after him, up the steps leading to the top of the fort.

Adam is already inside the tower when I duck through the little doorway and cram in next to him. We must look ridiculous, two grownups crouched inside the tower of a playground fort.

"Check out all the graffiti," Adam says, pointing to the vaulted ceiling above us. Every inch is covered in writing. There are a few English letters, many Kanji characters, numbers that seem to represent dates, and lots of hearts. Most of the hearts have large arrows below them, the tips touching the base of the heart. But they aren't supposed to be arrows …

I point to one. "Those are love umbrellas," I say.

"What?" he asks.

"A long time ago, men and women weren't supposed to be seen with each other in public, unless they were family members. The exception was on a rainy day, when a man could offer to share his umbrella with a woman if she didn't have one herself. Today, couples draw umbrellas and put their names underneath as a symbol of their love." As much I hate graffiti, the story behind these drawings makes me smile. Adam smiles too.

Suddenly, I remember the way his body felt pressed against me last night. Part of me wishes we could do that again right now, even though the thought of where it could lead us terrifies me.

Adam looks into my eyes. "So, what's next?"

My heart races. "What do you mean?"

He turns away from me and stares out of one of the tower windows for a moment before he finally says,

"What's on our itinerary for today?"

"My mom wanted to go to the 45th floor of the Metropolitan Government Office Building. On a clear day, you can see Mount Fuji from there, but I guess with all the clouds we probably won't see much."

"Only one way to find out." Adam brushes past me and zips down the slide.

I sit at the top of the slide, holding onto the bar to keep myself securely in place, watching Adam walk away. And then I slide to the ground.

Chapter Three

Judging by the roped-off elevator queue for the Metropolitan Government Office Building observation deck, this attraction is usually much more popular than it is today. That makes sense. Who wants to go to an observation deck on a cloudy day?

The elevator doors open and the attendant invites all of the people in the queue to pack inside the tiny space. I feel a twinge of discomfort deep in my throat. Ever since Barry, even an accidental unwanted touch can be excruciating, like I am being cut with a knife. I squeeze my palms together and slip in next to the elevator door, opposite the attendant. Adam steps in next to me, and I feel my tension ease.

The elevator makes no stops on the way to the 45th floor, but the ride feels far from fast. My breaths quicken as people shift position, coming dangerously close to me. Adam's presence is the only thing that keeps me from descending into panic.

When the doors finally open, we enter a bright room that stretches the entire length and width of the tower. There are huge windows in every direction. I finally take a deep breath, glad the elevator ride is over, at least for now.

On the wall above one of the windows, there's a photo of the view on a clear day, the view that my mom was no doubt hoping to see. Mount Fuji is visible in the photo, but when I look out the window, I see mostly grey clouds. Still, even the small part of Tokyo that is visible looks vast.

Adam and I move from window to window, checking out the diverse collection of skyscrapers and squat neighborhoods that look different from the ones back home. The skyscrapers look more modern, and the neighborhoods look absolutely ancient.

At one window, Adam points down through the glass. "There's our park."

Among the miniature trees far below us, I can't see the bench where we sat or the fort we climbed, but it is definitely the park where we ate our first breakfast in Japan; I see the small bridge we crossed on our way here.

I smile at the recognition of something familiar in this foreign place.

I wonder if my mom is out there. I wonder if she ever was.

* * *

About an hour ago, I accidentally stepped in a puddle. Now

water sloshes around in my sneakers with each step. My quick-dry pants are soaked and stuck to my calves; they should dry fast once we get out of the rain, but we don't have anyplace out of the rain to go.

We have lost ourselves in a neighborhood of diminutive two-story apartments. Tiny shrines adorn some of the entryways. A small cat hides from the rain on the roof of a car parked in an open garage. It would be interesting to wander here if we weren't so wet and hungry.

We turn down an alleyway and pass a vending machine offering bottled drinks. Today we've seen plenty of drink vending machines in Tokyo, but I haven't seen a single vending machine that offers food. I wish I'd bought more food at the Family Mart this morning. All I have left from my purchase is a tiny box of chocolate. I'm about to pull the chocolate out of my backpack when, at the end of the alley, we come upon a larger street.

Adam points to a sliding door, flanked by flowering potted plants, with short curtains along the top. "That could be a restaurant. Want to try it?"

I'm too hungry to pass it up, and so I say, "All right."

We tentatively slide open the door and find a small, elegant dining room, paneled in rich, dark wood. Paintings depicting white-capped ocean waves decorate the walls. An aproned chef works in the open kitchen. Only one of the three dining tables is occupied; a grey-haired man and woman and a young boy sit there, sipping soup. A younger woman with her dark hair pulled up neatly into a bun clears the table next to them.

"*Irasshaimase!*" she calls out to us. She slips the dishes she has collected into a plastic basin and hurriedly joins us by the door. She says something in Japanese and gestures to a hand-written sign with six columns of Kanji letters. There are prices below each row. It must be the menu.

I am always nervous about ordering food at a restaurant, but I'm even more anxious about ordering food at a restaurant in Japan. Not only am I a vegetarian, I'm allergic to shrimp—so much so that I need to carry a syringe of epinephrine, in case I accidentally eat anything prepared with shrimp, to keep my throat from swelling shut.

"*Bejitarian?*" I use the Japanese word for "vegetarian" and hand the woman a little card that Setsko wrote for me Japanese explaining my diet and my allergies.

The waitress reads the card and then nods. She points to the menu and says something that I don't understand, but she's nodding agreeably.

"Okay?" Adam asks me, his eyes uncertain.

"*Hai,*" I say to both him and the waitress.

She turns her attention to Adam, I assume to take his order.

"*Osusume wa nanidesu ka?*" Adam asks her for a recommendation. Adam eats anything and everything, and so his plan for choosing his meals in Japan at places where we can't read the menu is to ask the waiter or waitress what they'd recommend and agree with whatever they say.

The woman points to something on the menu.

"*Hai*," Adam accepts.

I'm not sure whether we've actually ordered meals, but the woman invites us to find a seat. There are four seats along one side of the kitchen, where diners can watch food being prepared. Adam and I sit there rather than at a table. I like the side-by-side seating arrangement. I don't want to sit face-to-face with Adam right now. It feels like it would be awkward even though it was never awkward before.

We watch the chef toss ingredients into two large woks. He drops cut-up cabbage into one and a piece of fish into the other.

"It looks like you're getting fish," I say to Adam.

"And you're getting … cabbage," he responds, wrinkling his nose.

I'm not a big fan of cabbage, but I will eat whatever I'm given.

The waitress places a cup of steaming soup in front of each of us.

"*Arigato*," we say, in unison.

And then we are silent. We sip spoonful after spoonful of what I recognize to be miso soup. By the time our soup is gone, our meals arrive. Mine is a bowl of white rice, a plate of chopped cabbage in sauce, some pickled vegetables I can't identify, and two squares of tofu. I use my chopsticks to break off a piece of the tofu. *It's cold.* I don't like cold tofu, but I eat it anyway. I need my protein. Next I try the cabbage.

"Oh my gosh!" I say as soon as I swallow. "This is so … good!"

"Mine too," Adam says, stuffing another bite of fish into his mouth.

I eat bite after amazing bite of the cabbage, occasionally using some rice to clean my palate, so I can taste the full flavor of the cabbage all over again. I have no idea what the dish is called, and so I'll probably never get to have it again. I want to experience it fully.

Suddenly, a loud scream cuts through the near silence of the restaurant. I spin around and see the grey-haired old woman customer standing and shouting. I don't understand her words, but her voice is filled with pure terror. The waitress rushes into the dining room. The two women exchange quick, panicked shouts and the waitress races away. The old man pulls the little boy from his seat and crouches by the boy's side. The boy is clutching his throat, crying silently. In fact, strangely, the little boy doesn't make any sound at all.

"Do you think he's choking?" I ask Adam.

Adam looks at the child with concern. "I don't know."

"I took a class once … I learned the Heimlich Maneuver …" I say.

I get to my feet and walk toward the family, unsure of

what I will say or do when I get there. Once I'm close, I see that the little boy's lips and the skin around his mouth are a dusky purple color. His eyes are brimming with panic. He *must be* choking. And no one seems to know what to do.

I point to myself and then to the boy and say to the old man, "I'm going to help him."

The man seems confused by my words, but he gives a shaky bow.

My heart pounds and my body trembles as I kneel behind the boy and make a fist over his belly button. I grab my fist with my other hand and pull sharply up and in. If this works, whatever object he is choking on should come shooting out of his mouth.

Nothing happens.

Maybe I didn't do it right.

I brace my hip against the boy's back and pull again. And again. And again. And again. And then the little boy goes limp in my arms. My soul fills with dread. I lower him to the ground. His eyes are half-open. The entire area around his mouth is purple now. I hear desperate voices around me.

I learned how to help someone who is choking a long time ago, but I feel like it was yesterday.

I hear my instructor's voice echo in my head as if she is kneeling right next to me now, "The child has passed out, what do you do?"

"Open the mouth and check for a foreign body," I hear

a younger version of myself say confidently.

I open the mouth of the boy lying in front of me. There's something light brown in the back of his throat—a piece of inari sushi, I think. I pull it out.

"Good job! The problem is fixed," I hear my instructor say, "but the child isn't moving."

"I need to do CPR," I hear a younger me say.

I put my hands in the center of the boy's chest—one on top of the other—and push down, over and over, hard and fast. The little boy's ribs bend unnaturally each time I press. The boy just lies there, deathly still. My eyes fill with tears.

I won't let you die, little boy. I'm pumping your heart and I won't stop until you wake up. I will NOT give up. Please wake up.

The boy's face grimaces, and he lets out a gurgling cry. I pull my hands back and stare at him in shock. The grey-haired woman lifts the boy into her arms, bowing to me over and over, saying something in Japanese. There is love in her voice.

I wipe my eyes with my sleeve and get to my feet. Adam is standing next to me. He looks like he's about to say something, but he doesn't speak. He leads me back to our seats and we sit. I keep my trembling hands in my lap as I watch the little boy cuddle with the old woman. The boy looks completely fine now. As if nothing ever happened.

Two men wearing firefighter uniforms enter the dining room with the waitress. She leads them to the little boy, speaking rapidly as they walk. One firefighter pulls a stethoscope from his bag and listens to the boy's chest. The other puts a sticker attached to a wire on the boy's finger.

The waitress walks over to us.

"*Okanjo onegaishimasu.*" Adam asks her for the check.

The woman says something that starts with "*iie*"—which means "no"—but I can't make out the rest of it.

Adam shrugs with confusion. "*Wakarimasen.*"

"Free," the woman says.

"*Iie,*" Adam says, shaking his head and opening his wallet.

The waitress raises her hands in front of herself. "Free," she repeats. And then she bows and walks away.

I turn back toward the little boy as the firefighters check his blood pressure. The boy looks up at me and waves shyly. I smile and wave back.

"Let's go," I say to Adam.

Adam stands and we go to the door. The waitress slides it open for us, bowing as she does it.

We raise our umbrellas and step out into the rain. Pulses of red light emanate from the small fire truck parked in the street and swirl across the surrounding buildings. I walk until I can no longer sense the flashes of red. Then I open the outer pocket of my backpack, pull out a brown package, and unwrap the cellophane. I press the "open" tab, and the end of the box collapses to reveal gold-wrapped chocolates inside.

"Would you like one?" I ask Adam.

"No thanks," Adam says as if his mind is busy with something else.

I take out a single chocolate and then push the end of the box closed. It elegantly springs back into place through some neat feat of candy-box-engineering.

"You saved that kid's life!" Adam whispers.

"Fate saved his life," I say.

"Fate?"

"When I was thirteen, I went to the library to return a book. The woman at the return desk asked me if I wanted to take a babysitting class that day. She said the class had been full for weeks, but five minutes earlier, one of the students had called to cancel. I didn't have plans, so I went. That's where I learned what to do if someone is choking.

"Years later, we're wandering around Tokyo and we end up at a restaurant where a little boy starts choking. He didn't have time to wait for an ambulance to arrive. The brain can only go a few minutes without oxygen before it starts to die. That little boy needed help to be right there. And it was."

"So you think *fate* brought you to that restaurant?" Adam asks.

"Everything happens for a reason," I say.

Adam sighs. "I wish that were true."

"It *is* true," I say. *I need to believe that.*

Adam doesn't argue, but I know him well enough to know that he doesn't agree. His brain is very practical. He believes only what makes sense. I'd like to make sense of everything too, but, sometimes, logical explanations are just too painful. Why would a mother abandon her child? *Because she didn't love her child enough to stay.* Why would a guy who grew up by my side steal my innocence? *Because he didn't care about me.* Why would my dad hold a gun to his own head and pull the trigger? *Because sometimes life isn't worth living.*

Tears form in my eyes. I unwrap the chocolate that I've been holding in my hand. My fingers are so cold that it's not the least bit melted. I put it into my mouth, and its smooth, milky deliciousness takes over my senses. I feel warm all over, like someone is giving me the hug I so desperately need right now. And then, within seconds, the feeling is gone.

* * *

There's a statue outside Shibuya Station to honor a dog named Hachikō. Hachikō's owner worked as a university professor in Tokyo. The professor commuted to work by train. Every afternoon, at the exact time that the professor's train was scheduled to arrive, Hachikō would wait at Shibuya Station to meet him.

One day, the professor died while he was at work. Hachikō waited at the station that afternoon, but of course, the professor never arrived. Hachiko didn't give up. He returned to the station the next afternoon, and every afternoon after that until his own death nearly ten years later. Instead of believing that his owner had abandoned him, he waited for him … forever.

My mom wanted to see the Hachikō statue. It's on her bucket list. She wrote, "Pay my respects to Hachiko."

On a pedestal at the center of a tree-lined square outside Shibuya Station, Adam and I find the life-sized bronze statue of Hachikō. Drips of rainwater hang from Hachikō's jowls. With the sleeve of my jacket, I wipe the water from his face. Though his left ear droops down, he holds his head high. He looks both weak and strong, but his strength seems so much greater than his weakness.

Right now, I feel mostly weak.

* * *

When we get back to our hotel room, Adam offers to let me take the first shower, which is good because my energy is fading. It almost hurts to be awake.

Freshly showered, I come back into the bedroom to find Adam undressed and under the covers, reading a book.

"What happened to your clothes?" I ask, wondering if he's completely naked.

"They're wet," Adam says, gesturing to the chair

where he laid them to dry.

"Right." I crawl under the covers of my bed.

Adam gets up, wearing boxers. "I assume you won't be awake when I'm done with my shower, so I'll say goodnight now."

"Do I look that bad?" I ask.

"You just look tired."

"I am," I say. "Goodnight."

"Goodnight," Adam says, and then he disappears around the corner.

I bite my lip, wondering what the next eight days will bring.

And then I close my eyes.

Chapter Four

"Good morning. It's raining," Adam says, drawing his dripping-wet hand in from the open hotel room window.

As I rub the sleep from my eyes, he sits on the edge of his bed and pulls on fresh shorts.

"So, what are we doing today?" he asks me.

I haven't shared our full itinerary with Adam. *Not* sharing it with him was part of an agreement we made before we left New York.

If it were up to Adam, we would have no itinerary at all for our journey. We would just wander around Japan and let things happen spontaneously. But I came here to follow my mom's bucket list. And so we came up with a compromise. The first part of our agreement was that I wouldn't tell Adam what we were going to do until the day we were going to do it. And even then, I was supposed to tell him as little as possible. The second part of the agreement was that we would spend an hour of each day "wandering aimlessly."

"First up is Yoyogi Park," I say, as I pick out my clothes for the day. "We can either take the train there or walk."

"Let's walk!" Adam says, putting on his shirt.

"I supposed that doesn't count as our daily dose of wandering aimlessly?" I ask.

Adam sighs. "We'll see."

* * *

It isn't exactly aimless, but we sure are wandering. Even with the help of the maps in my guidebooks, it's hard to figure out exactly which way to go to get to Yoyogi Park. About half an hour ago, we found a park, but it turned out to be Shinjuku Park, not Yoyogi.

The rain has lessened to a not-entirely-unpleasant drizzle, and so I lower my umbrella as we walk through a neighborhood reminiscent of the one we explored yesterday. Above us, jumbles of telephone wires travel down the streets and alleyways. The small homes and apartments here are weathered into various shades of dull brown and grey, but many of the entryways are flanked with plants and flowers that offer bursts of pinks, reds, and greens in this otherwise dreary place.

A woman crosses ahead of us with her dog. In the dog's mouth is the handle of a purse. The dog is carrying the woman's purse for her! I am instantly reminded of Hachikō.

Adam smiles. "If you want, this can count as our daily wandering. This is great."

"Yeah, it is."

Still, I hope we find Yoyogi Park ... eventually.

* * *

The towering legs of the unpainted wooden torii gate at the entrance to Yoyogi Park are streaked with green moss, as if someone swiped them with a paintbrush dipped in lime-green paint.

Just before Adam and I cross under the gate, the ground below us transitions from black pavement to grey gravel. The fog-enveloped path ahead is marked by wooden lanterns. A white-clad old man with receding grey hair smoothes the wet gravel with a handcrafted broom made of twigs. A few minutes after we pass him, I look back and the old man has disappeared into the mist.

We continue walking until we arrive at the entrance to Meiji Jingu Shrine. Adam and I stand side-by-side at the purification trough and ladle cold water over our hands to cleanse them before we enter. After we finish washing, we pass under a torii gate that looks like an exact replica of the gate at the entrance to Yoyogi Park, only much smaller.

A thick wooden doorway leads into the main courtyard. We lower our umbrellas and stroll the covered walkway that encircles the perimeter. The wood creaks softly under our feet. Drizzles of rain plummet from the roof. We occasionally cross paths with other visitors, but most of the time we're by ourselves until we arrive at a row of large, unglassed windows. People stand facing the windows. They bow, clap, toss coins, and close their eyes to say their prayers. I study them.

On my mom's bucket list was "Say a prayer at Meiji Jingu Shrine." That is why I'm here.

"I'll be right back," I whisper to Adam.

He nods.

I step forward and do what I saw those before me do. I toss a few coins into the long trough, bow twice in quick succession, clap my hands together twice, close my eyes, and recite the prayer that I prepared for this moment: *I don't know what my mom wanted to pray for here. But whatever that prayer was or whatever that prayer would have been. That's my prayer.*

I give another bow and then rejoin Adam.

It has stopped raining, and so we head into the courtyard where a thick, old tree is encircled by a low wall. Hundreds of small wooden plaques hang from pegs in the wall. Each plaque is decorated with handwritten words; a few also include hand-drawn pictures. Most of the words are in Kanji, although a few plaques are inscribed in English, and some in Spanish.

My hand reaches out to a stack of plaques at chest

level. I lift the first one, running my fingers over the Kanji letters that I can't read. I slide the plaque to the side to reveal the one beneath it; the words on this plaque are in English: "I wish for a happy marriage." I sift through the stack of plaques, feeling as though I'm looking for something that I can't find. The final plaque in the stack has writing in English, along with a child's drawing of a girl surrounded by hearts; the neatly-printed words say: "I wish I could be happy again."

I gently let the stack go and continue walking beside the wall. There must be hundreds of plaques hanging here right now, but over the course of many years, there must have been millions more inscribed by visitors. *What happened to the plaques that are no longer here?* Have they been thrown away? Or burned? Or buried?

"Erin, look!" Adam says.

I turn away from the wall and see tourists gathering to watch a procession of people wearing white robes layered over reds and purples. An unusually-large, bright-red umbrella shades a woman cloaked in a thick white hood and white robe. There is a bulge at her back, almost as if she's wearing a backpack beneath her clothing. Next to her is a man in a long black jacket and a striped kilt-like thing that hangs all the way down to his ankles.

"What is going on?" I ask no one in particular, because I don't expect that anyone will understand me.

"Wedding," a Japanese man with a camera trained on

the procession says, averting his gaze from his subject for just a split second.

When I was a little girl, I used to imagine what it would be like to get married. I pictured myself wearing a flowing white dress that dipped off each shoulder and a lacy veil that formed a white haze around my face. I imagined stepping slowly down a path sprinkled with rose petals to my groom in his suit with tails. I wonder if this woman under the big red umbrella imagined this moment when she was little. I wonder if she is happy. Her face doesn't give any hints.

As the procession passes us and the onlookers disperse, it starts to sprinkle again. I pull up the hood on my jacket to hide the tears forming in my eyes. Adam pulls up the hood on his own jacket. And we walk on through the mist.

Chapter Five

The path we take out of Yoyogi Park deposits us in Harajuku. "Go shopping in the narrow alleyways of Harajuku" was on my mom's bucket list, but the buildings we encounter are sleek and modern, a sharp contrast to the unique little shops I'd thought we would find here.

I pull off my hood because the rain has stopped—at least temporarily—and we duck down the first alleyway we see. Suddenly, the Harajuku I was expecting unfolds before us.

Small cafes are interspersed among stores selling unusual wares, like rainbow-colored tutus. Two women pass us wearing frilly, pink-and-blue dresses paired with tights covered in pastel hearts. Their outfits look like they belong on dolls rather than grownups. A few people have dyed hair, so, instead of a sea of jet-black-haired people, there are varying shades of reddish-brown-haired heads mixed in. Adam's blond hair and my light-brown hair still stand out though.

"Mind if we go in here?" Adam asks me, pointing to a shop whose window displays stone creatures that appear to be hawking stationary items, pens, and notebooks. "My mom would love that fox statue."

"Okay." I stare at the little stone fox, overwhelmed by the sudden feeling of emptiness in my stomach. I would give anything to have a mom to buy a gift for.

"*Irasshaimase!*" an older woman exclaims as we enter her store.

The shop is so tiny that it doesn't take long to browse the entire place. There are handcrafted greeting cards, postcards, and a small display of books. I lift a book with a white-capped wave hand-painted on the cover and open it. The pages inside are blank. The price is only 500 yen, and so I decide to buy it to satisfy the Harajuku entry on my mom's bucket list. It will make a nice gift for Setsko to thank her for all her help planning our trip

I take the book to the shopkeeper and place money in the little tray on the counter. The woman carefully wraps the book in a white paper bag and seals it with a gold sticker shaped like a fox.

"*Arigato*," I say.

"*Arigato gozaimasu*," she says.

Adam is right behind me. "What'd you get?"

"A notebook for Setsko," I say.

Adam places the fox statue on the counter.

I clutch my package to my chest and walk outside. It's

raining again. I tuck the notebook into my backpack and pull out my umbrella. Adam joins me a few seconds later.

"This looks like a good place to wander aimlessly," I say to him.

"I thought we already did that today," Adam says, peering down an alleyway.

"I'd like to do it again."

Adam smiles, but his smile is reserved; I think he can sense my sadness. "Okay."

Harajuku's maze of car-free streets is disorienting. I'm not sure how people ever find what they're looking for here. But now, getting lost is our goal. Each turn leads us somewhere new. Some streets are busy and hectic, while others are sleepy, with droopy trees, streetlights that are starting to illuminate even though it's still daytime, and cozy-looking apartments above the shops and cafes. If I lived in Tokyo, I might like to live above one of these streets.

On one quiet street is a clothing shop where, instead of mannequins, skinny teddy bears model the dresses. One bear wears a cute blue polka-dot sundress with a lacy collar. I didn't pack any dresses for our trip. I wonder if I should get one.

"I'd like to look in here," I say to Adam. I'm sure there's nothing in this store that would be of any interest to him, and so I offer, "Why don't we meet outside the store in fifteen minutes?"

"All right," Adam says. "I'll see you in fifteen."

I head inside the store and browse the dresses, each one more adorable than the next. I choose a few and then go to the back of the store where the shopkeeper is arranging a display of colorful barrettes by the register. I'm not sure how to ask to try on clothes, and so I show the dresses to the shopkeeper and then pantomime putting them on. She pulls back a baby-blue curtain printed with cartoon bears that hides a tiny closet with a long mirror, invites me to enter, and then closes the curtain behind me.

Inside the cramped dressing room, I take off my shorts and t-shirt and slip on the first dress; it catches at my hips. I try the next one. It won't fit either. The sizes must be different than I'm used to. I put my clothes back on and emerge. The shopkeeper looks at me expectantly.

"Wrong size," I say.

She looks me up and down and then says, "M," tracing the letter in the air with her finger.

I go back to the racks, trade my S's for M's, and return to the dressing room. This time, the first dress—the polka-dot sundress—goes on. I evaluate myself in the mirror. *I look like I'm about six years old. That won't work.* I slip the dress off and try on a lacy dress that I thought looked very feminine on the rack. I check myself out in the mirror. *I look like a tablecloth.* I quickly pull the dress off. The last dress that I try is covered with images of pink teddy bears—although, from a distance, they look like multicolored oval dots. It's the best one of the bunch, but I still look like a child who hasn't yet hit puberty. I hang the dresses back on their hangers and open the curtain, disappointed. The shopkeeper hustles over, holding out her hands.

I give her the dresses and shake my head. "*Iie.*"

"*Arigato gozaimasu,*" she says.

"*Arigato gozaimasu,*" I say.

I head back to the street, but Adam isn't there. It's still five minutes before we agreed to meet, and so I wander three stores away, to another dress shop. At the entrance, a human-sized cat mannequin is wearing a thigh-length, peach-colored dress decorated with Kanji characters. I don't know what the characters say, but I instantly fall in love with the dress. I find one with an "M" on the tag and take the dress to the back of the store.

The woman behind the counter shows me to a fitting room hidden behind a silky, multicolored curtain. I take off my clothes and pull the dress over my head. I can't help but smile at my reflection in the mirror. *It's perfect!* And then I check my watch. *I'm late!*

I leave the dress on, stuff my t-shirt and shorts into my backpack, pay the shopkeeper, and rush outside. I backtrack to the teddy-bear dress store, expecting to see Adam waiting for me. But he's not there. *Maybe he lost track of time too.*

Fifteen minutes later, I start to feel uneasy. Normally, I

would call Adam, but we don't have cellphones with us. Our U.S. cellphones are useless here and the cost to rent two cellphones that work in Japan wasn't in our budget. "Besides," I had said when we were planning our trip, "people once survived without cellphones." And so we agreed that we wouldn't need them. Now, on only our second day in Japan, we need them.

People swirl around me. The sky is getting darker.

He'll come back. I know he'll come back.

But he doesn't.

* * *

About an hour after I was supposed to meet Adam in front of the dress shop, it starts getting seriously cold. I pull out my jacket, slip it on over my brand-new dress, and walk up and down the small street a few times to try to get warm. Then it starts to rain.

Umbrellas pop into action all around me. I pull mine out too. Icy pricks stab my bare legs. I start to shiver. *I should go back to the hotel.* Eventually, that's where Adam will go too, I hope.

* * *

It was easier to find the train station than I thought it would be. Every time I lost my way, I asked someone, *"Eki wa doko desu ka?"* Then I followed the first direction that they pointed.

When I board the packed train, I don't bother looking for a seat. There's only one train stop between Harajuku and Shinjuku—Yoyogi Station—and so I decide to stand. I grab onto a pole next to a seated woman with a small girl on her lap. The girl wears a light-blue, overall-style dress with a white shirt; it could be a uniform, although she doesn't look old enough to be in school yet. The girl smoothes the hair of a Little Red Ridinghood doll that she holds close to her, as if it's her most precious possession.

A man leaps through the closing doors and squeezes in next to me. I do a double-take. Other than Adam, he's the only Caucasian person I've seen since we left the airport. He looks into my eyes and his lips curl into a small smile. My body tingles with trepidation. I don't trust him—not in the general way that I don't trust men anymore, but in a deep instinctual way.

When the train stops at Yoyogi Station, I consider getting off and waiting for the next train to Shinjuku—just to get away from the man, who is standing closer than feels appropriate—but Shinjuku Station is just a few minutes away. *I can do this.*

As the train approaches Shinjuku Station, people shift toward the door, but I wait. I don't want to give the man any indication of my plans. I feel the man's eyes on me, watching me, as if he is a predator and I am his prey.

The train slows to a stop and the door opens. People burst out. The woman next to me lifts the little girl into her arms and she hurries to the door. I follow them, imagining that the three of us are together so I don't feel so alone.

As we exit the train, a tiny blood-red cape flitters from the little girl's doll to the ground. I reach down and snatch the cape from the train floor. People wind around me, separating me from the woman and the girl. New people board the train; I squirm past them, fighting against the tide.

Once I'm on the platform, I exhale and scan the crowd. The woman and the little girl are already about twenty crowded feet away from me, and moving further away fast. I race to catch up with them, weaving in and out, dodging the people coming toward me, trying to close the distance. Once I'm close, I struggle to move into the woman's line of sight. I don't know if it's appropriate in Japan to touch someone's shoulder to get their attention. I have a feeling it isn't.

"*Sumimasen,*" I call out.

The woman glances in my direction, and I hold out the cape. I see a glint of recognition in the woman's eyes and in the eyes of the little girl. The woman deftly ducks out of the surging crowd and stops. I hand her the cape. She gives a small bow.

"*Arigato gozaimasu,*" she says.

I forget how to say "you're welcome" in Japanese, and so I just nod. The woman bows again and then continues on her way.

I feel a hand touch my arm. *Adam?* I turn toward the

hand.

The man from the train is standing next to me, smiling. My throat constricts. I step away from him and start walking. I feel him following me.

"That was very sweet what you just did," he calls out to me with a thick accent that I can't place.

I walk faster.

"Where are you from?" he asks, catching up with me.

"Sorry, I'm in a rush," I say to him.

The man grabs my arm, stopping me. "Don't be rude."

My heart pounds. I look into his eyes, trying to hide my fear. "Let go of me," I growl.

The man twists my arm behind my back. Pain surges through my shoulder as he pulls our bodies together. He leans close to my ear. I feel his rancid breath against my face. He says something, but I don't understand it. Everything sounds muffled: the crowd, the train, the man's deep voice.

Hot anger surges through me. "Get away from me!" I grit my teeth and jam the inside of my foot into the middle of his bare shin, scraping his leg. He twists my arm harder, forcing my chest against him. "GET AWAY!" I slam my free hand against his throat. The man gasps and buckles forward. His grip loosens. I thrust my knee into his groin.

And I run.

I don't turn back to see if I'm being followed. I don't want to know.

*　*　*

When I finally stand still inside the elevator at my hotel, I realize that I'm shaking. I spent the last few minutes running. To the end of the train platform. Down the stairs that lead into the station. To the station exit. Along the busy sidewalk. Down the lonely street where our hotel is. Through the hotel lobby. Into an empty waiting elevator.

Numbers blink on the small screen by the door as we pass each floor our way up. A female computer voice announces something in Japanese. Then the elevator stops and its doors open.

I peer down the deserted hallway. Then I step out of the elevator and make my way to my room. I check the hallway one more time to make sure it's empty before I put my keycard into the slot. The door pops open. The room is dark. The lights in the room won't operate unless a room key is inserted into the slot just inside the door. I had hoped that Adam's keycard would be there, and that he would be waiting in the room for me, but there's no key there. I slip my keycard into the slot, and a few lights illuminate.

I walk down the narrow hallway and scan the bedroom, looking for evidence that Adam has returned to the room since we left this morning. But there is no backpack. No jacket.

Adam should have been here by now. *Where else would he have gone?*

I drop my backpack onto a chair, followed by my jacket. I slip off my sneakers and sit on my bed, drawing my legs up close to my body. My hands feel warm against my cold damp shins. I rest my forehead against my knees, and finally give my tears permission to flow.

The door clicks. *Adam's here!* I wipe the tears from my eyes with the back of my hand and start to stand, but then I freeze. *What if it isn't Adam? What if the man from the train station followed me back to the hotel?* He could have convinced the people at the front desk that he'd been accidentally locked out of our room and asked them to give him a key.

BANG! Metal hits against metal as someone pushes the door open. BANG!

But no one enters the room. *I must have closed the security bar without even thinking.*

Someone knocks hard on the door. I creep into the hallway. They knock again, startling me even though I should have expected it.

"Erin." It's Adam's voice.

I go to the door. "Adam?"

Adam pokes his face into the small opening under the security bar. "Yeah."

"Hold on." I close the door, unlatch the security bar, and then open the door.

I hear Adam close the door and relock the security bar as I walk back to the bedroom. I sit on the edge of my bed.

Adam drops his backpack onto the floor and sits on my bed next to me.

"I'm sorry. I got turned around," he says. "I think I walked every street and alley in Harajuku before I finally found that dress shop again." And then he looks at me. "Are you okay?"

"A man grabbed me."

Adam squeezes his right hand into a fist. "I should never have left you alone."

"I hit him in the throat and kneed him in the groin," I say.

Relief floods Adam's face. "Good job," he whispers.

Many months ago, when I confided in Adam about what happened with Barry, I mentioned how helpless I'd felt; I'd wanted to fight Barry off, but I didn't know how to defend myself against someone so big and strong. The next day, Adam found a women's self-defense class for me to take. I refused to go. The thought of having some stranger pretend to attack me made my skin prickle. And so Adam rented a self-defense video from the library. He watched it with me. And then we practiced together. That was the first time he ever physically touched me. He touched me, and I fought him off. And then he touched me again, and I fought him off. It was the only kind of touch I could accept at that time, a touch I could fight off. That's how I learned the techniques I used on the train platform.

Adam and I stare at each other intensely, as if we

might kiss, but before we do, I look away. "I got to our meeting spot about ten minutes after we were supposed to meet there," I admit. "I thought you left without me."

Adam's right hand unclenches and takes mine. "I would *never* willingly abandon you," he says. Deep down inside me, I know that is true.

I lean back onto the bed and pull Adam against me, holding him desperately.

Slowly, our bodies entangle.

Chapter Six

Adam and I spent the entire night in each other's arms, our hands never straying to places on each other that friends aren't supposed to touch. But we haven't touched since we disentangled ourselves early this morning.

The first leg of our nearly three-hour train trip from Tokyo to Nikko was on one of Japan's famous bullet trains. Adam read a book while I gazed out the window, watching gray cities give way to lush, green countryside. The second leg of our trip was on a small local train where we sat facing an older gentleman who doodled in his notebook as the train bounced in a gentle rhythm along the tracks.

As we pull into the train station in Nikko, I steal a glimpse of the old man's notebook just before he closes it. I stifle a gasp. On the page where I'd thought that he'd been mindlessly doodling is a sketch so rich in detail that it looks like a black-and-white photo. It shows a footbridge stretching over a turbulent river in a forest. The sketch's haunting beauty stays with me, even once the drawing is out of sight.

The old man exits the train before us. We follow him through the train station. He leads us to the exit. Once we are outside the station, I'm struck by how unlike Tokyo this town is. It's quiet and slow here. Mountains loom in the distance, their tops shrouded in clouds. We walk up the first street we come to, where shops spill their unique personalities onto the sidewalks. Nothing looks very modern, and nothing is more than three-stories high.

"Are we following that guy?" Adam asks, gesturing toward the old man from the train, who is about thirty seconds ahead of us.

"Of course not. That would be creepy, right?" I say, but then I realize how much I want to know where this man is going.

Adam eyes me. "Not if there were a good reason ..."

The old man turns down a street on the left, I keep after him.

"Did you see what he was drawing on the train?" I whisper.

"No."

"It was like looking at a photograph."

Adam looks amused. "That's your reason?"

"Yeah."

Adam shrugs. "All right."

The man turns and enters a building. When we arrive

at the spot where he disappeared, we find the curtained entrance to what appears to be a restaurant.

"Hungry?" I ask Adam.

Adam looks at the exterior walls of the building—which are coated with peeling dark-green paint—and the uninspiring plain white curtain hanging across the doorway; these are our only clues to what lies inside.

He looks back at me. "The guy's probably a local. Maybe the food here is really good."

I smile. "Okay?"

"Okay," Adam says, and then he slides open the door and ducks under the curtain.

The restaurant is rather homely on the inside too. The décor is a mismatched collection of old photos and garish paintings and sculptures. I'm surprised that the old man—who is obviously a brilliant artist—doesn't find the surroundings completely unappetizing. Apparently he does not, because he's seated at a small table tucked away in the corner—near a particularly off-putting sculpture of some sort of mythical creature—ordering something from the waitress.

The old man is the restaurant's only customer. I start to reconsider eating our lunch here, but the waitress is already shuffling over to greet us. She gestures widely to the dining room, offering us our choice of tables. Adam and I quickly choose one.

As soon as we are seated, the woman hurries over at a

much faster pace than I'd expected she was capable of. She holds a menu out in front of her face and says, "English ... menu."

"*Arigato gozaimasu.*" Adam takes the menu and passes it to me.

The food choices *are* listed in English, sort-of. Some of the descriptions are a bit confusing, but most of the items have a small photo as well to offer assistance. I decide on the curry udon and hand the menu to Adam. While Adam looks it over, I steal another look at the old man. He's drawing in his sketchbook again, stopping only to acknowledge the waitress who brings him a steaming bowl of something.

The man ignores whatever the woman placed on his table, instead focusing on his sketch. His strokes are small and delicate. I wonder if he's still working on the bridge drawing or if he has moved on to something new.

The waitress approaches us.

"Ready?" Adam asks me.

"Yeah." I turn to the waitress and point to the curry udon photo in the menu.

The waitress says something in Japanese. I nod, even though I have no idea what she said. She directs her attention to Adam. He points to a different photo. She says something to him too; this time I recognize the Japanese word for shrimp: "*ebi.*" I made sure to learn the Japanese word for the one food that could kill me. Adam did too.

"*Ebi?*" he asks her.

"*Hai*," she says.

"The description didn't say anything about shrimp," Adam says to me.

"It's okay," I say, "I won't be eating it. And I have my EpiPen just in case."

"*Iie*," Adam says, making an "X" with his arms—a gesture that Setsko taught us as a way to communicate "no." He points to a different meal.

"*Hai*," she says, along with something else in Japanese.

I should probably make sure that my meal doesn't come with any unwelcome surprises. Feeling self-conscious, I pull out my little diet explanation card and point to the sentence that says I'm allergic to shrimp.

"*Hai*," the waitress says. She holds her arms up, making an "X," and says, "*Ebi* no."

"*Arigato gozaimasu*," I say.

She bows and walks off, taking the menu with her.

"You didn't have to change your choice for me," I say to Adam.

"It's not worth the risk," he says, looking down at my hand resting on the table. He touches the tips of his fingers to the tips of mine so quickly and so lightly that the instant he's done I'm not sure that he touched me at all.

I stare at our hands, now inches away from each other, until I get the sensation that we're being watched. As I look up toward the old man, I see him lower his head to his drawing.

The old man was watching us.

* * *

The delicious spices of my curry udon still linger in my mouth when the waitress places the check on our table.

"Do you think they have a restroom here?" I ask Adam.

"I would guess so," Adam says.

Ordinarily I would think so too, but the dining room is small, and there are only two doors: the door that leads to the street and the curtained doorway from which the waitress appeared with our food.

"*Toire wa?*" I ask the waitress.

"*Hai.*"

She leads me to the cash register, pushes aside the curtain behind it, and invites me to enter a hallway even narrower than the one in our hotel room. There's another curtain along the wall—maybe hiding the entrance to the kitchen. Then the hallway turns. There are no lights here. I feel like I could be heading to my doom.

The woman opens a wooden door to a closet-sized room barely big enough for the toilet inside. There isn't even a sink to wash my hands.

She turns on a light inside the toilet room.

"*Arigato,*" I say, and I shut myself inside.

I notice what looks like a tiny sink built into the top of the toilet tank. I wonder if it works. When I press the flush button, I get the answer; as the toilet flushes, water flows from the toilet sink's spout. I wash my hands until the water trickles to a stop.

Like most of the restrooms in Japan, there are no paper towels available here. Most people carry a wash-cloth-sized towel with them everywhere they go. Adam and I each bought one at our hotel's gift shop, but I left mine in my backpack at the table.

I open the door with wet hands, and retrace my path back to the dining room. Adam is waiting at our table. He's smiling.

"What?" I ask.

"Nothing," Adam says, collecting his backpack.

Before we leave, I take a final look back to the corner of the restaurant, thinking that I might nod goodbye to the old man, even though we never met.

But the man is gone.

* * *

I have a small map of Nikko that I drew based on a map in one of my guidebooks. I left the guidebooks at the hotel because I wanted to travel lighter today. My back is starting to feel sore, probably because I've been holding it so tense, but the extra weight of the guidebooks in my backpack certainly wasn't helping.

I wish I'd included more details on my map. I feel like we've been walking along this road much longer than we should have without reaching our destination.

"What are we looking for?" Adam asks.

He must be sensing my uncertainty.

"Two bridges," I say. "A plain one and a fancy one."

Adam smiles. "So what did your mom write on her list about the bridges?"

"The bridges aren't on her list. They're just my landmarks."

We round a bend and Adam points. "Those bridges?"

Ahead of us is a short, ordinary-looking bridge. A car drives slowly across it. A few feet away, almost parallel to the first bridge, is a vermillion-colored wooden footbridge.

"Yes!" I skip ahead until I land in the center of the plain bridge.

The other bridge—Shinkyo Bridge—gently arches over a boulder-strewn white patch of the otherwise placid blue-green river. One end of Shinkyo Bridge is blocked off, and so it can't be used to cross the river; tourists can pay to walk across the bridge, but they must then turn around and cross back the way they came.

I lean against the railing and look down at the river flowing beneath us. A thin layer of fog hangs over the water. I can almost feel its chill. I shudder, realizing what I was thinking: *What would it feel like to jump off this bridge?* I used to have thoughts like that a lot about a year ago, but I haven't had them for a while. I lift my gaze and stare at Shinkyo Bridge until I feel normal again.

And then I realize something: "That bridge is what the man on the train was sketching." It's as if his sketch has suddenly come to life, in color.

Adam puts something in my hand. *The old man's sketch.*

"Where did you get this?" I ask.

"The man gave it to me as he was leaving. He put it on the table and said, 'For her.' I offered him money, but he wouldn't accept it."

I hold up the sketch, comparing it to the bridge. It's a perfect match. "Why did he want to give it to me?"

"I guess he thought you would like it."

"I love it." I stare at the sketch for a while before I carefully tuck it into my backpack. Then we start upstream, letting the river be our guide until I see a sign that directs us to turn away from water and into the fog-enveloped forest.

* * *

Weathered stone lanterns tower over us like abandoned pieces from a giant's game of chess played out in a mystical forest. Many of their crowns are covered in a thick layer of moss. Some of them have lush ferns springing from their tops. I don't imagine that the ferns were planted there; they found their way there on their own.

The nearby buildings that make up Toshogu Shrine are

exquisitely ornate. Their intricately-carved wooden exteriors are painted in reds, greens, and blues, with golden accents. Japanese shrines aren't known for their opulence; Toshogu Shrine is a rare exception.

Strangely, I'm drawn to a plain wooden structure. The weathered wood matches the color of the tall tree trunks that serve as its backdrop. The only significant decoration of the simple shack is a narrow row of carved, painted panels. On the panel above me are the images of three monkeys. One monkey covers his ears, the second covers his mouth, and the third covers his eyes.

"That's the original depiction of the three wise monkeys," I say to Adam. "It's something my mom had on her list."

Adam grins, looking at the monkeys. "Hear no evil. Speak no evil. See no evil."

I gesture to the other panels. "I read in my guidebooks that the panels illustrate the journey from babyhood to adulthood. I'm not sure if my mom had any interest in the meaning behind the carvings. Or if she even knew about their story."

Adam moves to the first panel. It shows two monkeys, a small one and a bigger one. The monkeys inhabit a forest filled with colorful, exotic flowers. The big monkey has one paw on her forehead, as if she's searching for something in the distance. The little monkey looks up at the big one, as if asking for guidance.

"Tell me the story," Adam requests as I join him.

"In the first panel, the mother monkey is looking into her baby's future."

We continue past the other panels, stopping to admire each one as I tell Adam its meaning. "As a child, the monkey hears no evil, speaks no evil, and sees no evil. The little monkey grows independent and develops ambitions. She gets encouragement from her friends. Once she's all grown up, she falls in love and gets married ..."

"How do you know it's a *she*?" Adam asks.

I point to the final panel. "In that one, she's pregnant."

Adam goes to the panel and studies it. "Why is she all alone there?"

I stare at the swollen belly of the lone, pregnant monkey. A lump forms in my throat. "I don't know."

* * *

Adam and I stand, shoeless, in a dimly-lit room with a bunch of strangers, staring up at a painting of a dragon on the ceiling. A monk speaks to us, entirely in Japanese, but I think I know what's about to happen. On my mom's bucket list, under Toshogu Shrine, the second thing she wrote was, "Hear the dragon cry."

After some research, I discovered that there's a building at Toshogu Shrine that has a special property: when something is clapped together inside it, the sound is supposed to resemble a dragon's cry. In the monk's hands are two blocks of wood.

The monk holds the blocks above his head and bangs them purposefully together. It sounds like … two blocks of wood being banged together. I look at Adam who appears puzzled.

The man takes a few steps and then bangs the blocks again. This time, the sound is decidedly different. It sounds a bit like the combination of a cat's purr and meow. It doesn't resemble a sound that I think a dragon would make under any circumstances, but it's definitely a different sound than the clapping together of two blocks of wood. He slaps the blocks together one more time to prove his point. And then says something. Judging by the behavior of the other tourists, he has dismissed us.

Adam and I follow the crowd through the gift shop and out the main door.

"Okay, I give up. What was with the wooden blocks?" Adam asks me.

"The last two times sounded different than the first time, right?" I ask him.

"Yeah."

"It was supposed to sound like the cry of a dragon."

Adam smiles. "It sounded more like a cat to me."

I laugh. "I thought so too."

Raindrops pelt the nearly-deserted concrete pathways that weave between the shrine buildings. We collect our shoes and sit on the steps of the building, under an overhang, to put them on. Then we pull up our hoods and start walking past the weathered stone lanterns and lavishly-painted buildings. As we arrive at a tall torii gate, the rain slows to a stop. I can't resist the opportunity to get a photo of myself with the gate and no other tourists in the background.

I hand Adam my camera. "Can you take a picture of me here?"

"Sure." He walks back far enough to get the torii gate in the photo and snaps a picture.

We trade cameras and I take a matching photo of him.

"I wish we could get a picture of us together," I say. "But there's no one around to take our photo."

"No problem. Come with me," he says.

I follow Adam away from the gate. Every once in a while, he glances back toward it. Finally, he holds out his camera, leans close to me, and says, "One, two, three."

He turns the camera around and shows me a perfectly-framed photo of us with the torii gate in the background.

"That's awesome," I say. "Thanks."

Adam looks into my eyes. I feel like he wants to kiss me. But then his gaze shifts back to his camera. He stuffs it into his bag and then starts along the path toward the exit. I exhale silently and follow.

* * *

I drop my backpack into the chair next to Adam's and

collapse onto my bed. "My back's so sore," I mutter.

"Did you injure it?" Adam asks.

"I think it's from wearing my backpack so much and being so tense."

"Want a massage?"

Before I fully consider my answer, I roll onto my stomach and say, "Okay."

I feel Adam put one leg on either side of my hips. He takes my shoulders in his hands and squeezes. Warmth washes over me. He presses his fingers into my muscles. Pleasure envelops my body. I try to ignore the tingling that radiates from my shoulders to my chest as Adam moves down along my spine, gently pinching the muscles as he goes. I take a deep breath, but I don't let it out. I need that breath to keep my body still.

"You're good at this," I murmur.

"I took a class once."

"It was a very good class." The words spill out of my mouth.

"Why have you been so tense?" he whispers.

"Huh?"

"You said you've been tense."

I regret starting a conversation. I take another deep breath, trying to get enough oxygen to my brain to come up with an answer to his question. "Everything's so different here."

"Isn't that what traveling is all about?"

"Everything's different with *us* too." I roll over. Adam raises his body to accommodate me and then lowers it again. He pulls my shirt down to cover my exposed belly, even though he doesn't seem to want to. I look into his eyes. "I feel like we're more ... intimate."

He rests his hands on my shoulders. "Is that a bad thing?"

"No, it's good. I like it."

"I like it too," he says, with a barely perceptible sigh.

Adam begins to massage my shoulders from this new position, his fingers working into the back of my neck. I close my eyes.

Chapter Seven

When I wake up, I'm fairly certain that it's morning. I open my eyes and check the clock. It's eight AM. I look at Adam's bed. He isn't there. *He's probably in the bathroom.*

I turn on my bedside light and pull out my mom's bucket list. Today, Adam and I will be heading to Kamakura—a small town about one hour's train ride from Tokyo. Under Kamakura, my mom wrote:

Great Buddha of Kamakura
● Go inside the Buddha.

Zeniarai-Benzaiten Shrine
● Wash money in the lucky water and then spend it.

Hase Temple

- Explore the cave that honors
a sea goddess.

Adam still hasn't come out of the bathroom, and I really need to pee, so I slip out from under my covers and walk to the bathroom.

I tap on the door. "Adam?"

There's no answer.

I knock louder. "Adam?"

I try the door. It opens. No one's inside the bathroom. *Where is Adam?*

I pee, and then I go back to the bedroom to check for a note. I look on his bed. On mine. On the floor. On the chair. I open the curtains and check the counter by the window. I go back into the bathroom and check the mirror. And the sink.

I finally conclude that there is no note.

I decide to get ready for the day. If Adam isn't back by the time I'm done, I'll go looking for him. He probably went to the hotel lobby to read his book, so he wouldn't disturb me.

The room feels too quiet, and so I turn on the TV and let the morning news be my soundtrack as I brush my teeth and wash my face. Before I choose my outfit, I open the window and stick out my hand to check for rain; my hand comes back dry. I get dressed, organize my backpack, and then I'm ready.

I pick up the pad of paper on the nightstand. And I write:

Adam,

It's 8:45. I went to go look for you. If I don't find you, I'll come back to the room at 9:15.

Erin

The door clicks open. Adam enters the room briskly and brushes past me. "Hey," he says.

I tear the page off the pad, crumple it up, and toss it in the trashcan. "Hey. Where were you?"

"I'm sorry. I didn't think I'd be gone that long." He sits on his bed. His face looks ashen.

I sit down next to him. "What's wrong?"

Adam drops his forehead into his hand and presses against it with his fingers. "I need some air. Are you ready to go?"

"Yeah," I say.

Adam gets up and grabs his backpack.

I follow him out the door.

* * *

There's a civilized way to travel to the Great Buddha of Kamakura, Zeniarai-Benzaiten Shrine, and Hase Temple, via paved roads, but the simplest way to visit all three places is by hiking a rugged dirt trail called Daibutsu Hiking Course. I think my mom would have chosen to take the trail if she knew about it. Maybe she did.

Daibutsu Hiking Course starts near Jochiji Temple—which is close to Kita-Kamakura train station. When we get off the train, we cross a stone footbridge over a turtle-inhabited pond lined with thick green foliage and then walk along the edge of a two-lane road, following the signs to Jochiji Temple. There are no sidewalks here, but the cars and trucks are traveling so slowly that it feels fairly safe.

At Jochiji Temple, we find a worn road that turns into a skinny trail that leads up the hillside. I feel nervous about leaving what little civilization there is here in Kamakura behind, but I start ascending.

Adam hasn't said much since we left the hotel room. He spent the entire one-hour train ride from Shinjuku to Kamakura staring out the window rather than reading, which is very out of character for him. Obviously he's troubled about something, but I'm not sure what it is. The massage he gave me last night seemed to go well. Afterward, I offered to give him one, and he said he'd take a rain check. Then we both took showers and went to bed.

Adam seemed fine. What happened between then and now?

The path levels out into a dirt trail. Erosion has exposed the serpentine roots of many of the trees, creating a scene that's both eerie and enchanting. When I was a toddler, my mother and I used to go on nature walks like this with my best friend and his mom. I don't remember those walks, but I have pictures. They are some of the few pictures I have of my mom. And they are some of the last.

The trail opens up into a small park. A lone monk—clad in all white, except for his black rain boots—rakes the gravel in front of a stone torii gate hung with white folded-paper decorations. *I wonder if this is the money-washing shrine.* The only person around to ask is the monk—and it doesn't feel right to disturb him—so we wander past him into the shrine. A stone walkway leads past bushes blooming with hydrangeas in various shades of pink, purple and blue to a pair of large rocks, one smaller and one larger, joined by a rope to which so many little red strings have been tied that it looks like the rope itself is bright red. It isn't though. By one of the knots I see a small hint of gold rope beneath the red strings. Tied to the red strings are coins—offerings I suppose. Surrounding the rocks are walls of prayer plaques, like the ones at Meiji Jingu Shrine, except that these plaques are heart shaped. *This must be a shrine dedicated to love.*

Adam has wandered to the far end of the shrine, where he is taking photos of a stone fox. I push some money into a little offering box by the blank prayer plaques and take a plaque. I grab a marker and place my fingers on the cap, thinking about what I will write on my plaque. Since this is a love shrine, I should write a prayer about love. I am about to write: *I wish to find my soulmate.* But then I wonder if maybe I've already found him. And I just can't have him.

Adam starts back down the path, heading toward me. I hang my blank prayer plaque on the wall with the other people's plaques and return the marker unopened.

Adam looks at me, with tired eyes that show a hint of curiosity. "What'd you write?"

"Nothing," I say.

"Fine, don't tell me," he says.

"I didn't write anything. I left it blank." I touch my blank plaque, and Adam's forehead furrows.

"Why'd you leave it blank?" he asks.

"Because I wasn't sure what to write."

I turn and head back to the shrine entrance. The monk is gone. I cross the freshly-raked gravel and approach a family who is setting up a picnic.

"Zeniarai-Benzaiten Shrine?" I ask the woman, hoping she'll offer directions to the money-washing shrine.

"*Hai,*" she says. And then she says something more, pointing as she speaks. I focus on the movements of her hands.

"*Arigato,*" I say when she's through.

Adam and I descend in the first direction that the

woman pointed—via a steep stairway—and then in the second direction that she indicated—down a narrow road. The road is so curvy that I can't see very far ahead. Each bend leads to another until we find ourselves among a large group of grade-schoolers in sailor-inspired school uniforms milling about near a stone torii gate that stands before a tunnel cut into a fern-covered wall of rock.

The tunnel reminds me of the one that Chihiro and her family pass through in the animated Japanese film *Spirited Away*. Adam and I watched that film on the day we decided to go to Japan. After the film was over, I told Adam that my mom dreamed about going to Japan and that I couldn't get the feeling that I needed to go there out of my head. That's when Adam suggested that we go to Japan together. Somehow, it didn't seem like such a crazy idea, and I agreed. Before we could reconsider, Adam opened up his laptop and booked our plane tickets.

Like in the movie, at the other side of this tunnel is what feels like a different world. I follow Adam onto a quiet stone path that winds its way among small shrines.

"What did your mom want to do here?" Adam asks as we stop to admire a small shrine guarded by a stone creature that looks like a cross between a lion and a dragon.

"There's a cave with a stream where you can wash your money. And then when you spend that money, it's supposed to bring you luck."

"And at that last shrine?"

"I don't think she knew about that shrine," I say. "It wasn't on her list." Although, I think she would have liked it.

We stroll among the mini-shrines until we find the jagged rocky entrance to the money-washing cave. Colorful chains of origami hang from the roof of the cave; some have been hanging there so long that their colors have begun to fade. I watch an old woman, with white streaks in her short grey hair, carefully place some bills into a wicker basket. She holds the basket over the stream and uses a silver ladle with a wooden handle to proficiently pour water over the money; it looks as if this is something she does every day. When she is through, she collects her money and walks away.

Adam and I take all of the money from our wallets. I choose a basket and lay my money inside. Adam puts his money next to mine. I'd expected him to take his own basket, but I like that he wants to share just one. I squat down and ladle water over the money. Adam stands by my side.

"You should do it too," I say, offering him the ladle.

Adam squats beside me, scoops up some water, and slowly pours it over the coins and bills as if it's the most important thing in the world that every bit of the money be saturated. He takes another scoop of water and pours it just as deliberately. Then he returns the ladle to the rack.

Without a word, we collect our soggy money from the

basket and put it in our wallets. Then we walk back through the tunnel, climb the winding road, and rejoin the hiking trail.

The next part of the trail is muddier than the first part. My sneakers slide a little. Adam takes my hand to steady me and keeps it.

"I'm sorry I've been so quiet," Adam says. "I have a lot on my mind."

I turn toward him, but he doesn't return my gaze.

"Whatever it is," I say, "if you want to talk about it, I'm here."

Adam stops walking. He seems to need every bit of his energy to try to force his next words out. And then he finally does. "Natsumi is pregnant."

Chapter Eight

If I stand still, I think I will pass out. So I start walking, focusing straight ahead. I don't look at Adam—I don't want him to see the shock in my eyes. Questions spring to my lips, but I hold them back.

"This morning I got an email from Michelle," Adam says. "She's a friend of mine from highschool."

"Why didn't Natsumi email you?" I ask.

"Michelle said that Natsumi wasn't planning to tell me about the baby."

My foot slips on the mud. Adam tightens his grip on my hand to stop me from falling.

"Are you sure you're the father?" I ask.

"Yes."

"What are you going to do?"

He takes a deep breath. "The kid is going to need a dad in their life. I'm going to be the kid's dad."

And there it is: the only solution I could ever imagine

Adam considering.

"How far along is she?" I ask.

"About six months."

In three months, Adam is going to be a father to another woman's baby.

That thought breaks my heart.

* * *

Being inside the Great Buddha of Kamakura feels suffocating, but that might be because my head has felt fuzzy and my chest tight ever since Adam told me his secret.

The inner walls of the Buddha are a bumpy mix of bulges and seams where the different plates that make up the statue fit together. It reminds me of the inside of the Statue of Liberty, but smaller and cruder. There's something compelling about their raw imperfectness.

Along every seam within the reach of human hands, coins have been balanced precariously; it looks like it would take just a tap on the wall to cause all of them to tumble. The majority of the coins are arranged along the front wall, above metal plaques engraved with Kanji letters. I stare at the letters—tiny pictures—like little works of art—arranged in orderly columns. I wonder if they form a prayer, or information about the history of this statue, or something else.

And then I notice that, scratched into the paint on the

wall beside the plaques, there are more Kanji letters. These letters are skinny and ugly: graffiti—like the graffiti inside the tower of the playground fort. But there are no hearts or arrows in this graffiti, just letters. Do they form names? Or prayers? *What was so important to say that someone had to scratch it into the walls of this special place? How dare they do that?* I wish I could scrape away all of the graffiti and make the wall clean again, but I can't. I can't fix this. I turn away from the wall; I can't look at it anymore without feeling helpless.

Adam is standing by the stairway that leads to the outside. I walk directly to him, but he doesn't seem to see me until I brush his arm.

"You all right?" I ask.

"I'm feeling claustrophobic," Adam says.

"I didn't know you were claustrophobic," I say.

"I'm not."

Adam turns and heads down the staircase to the exit. I follow him, and we emerge in the daylight. The gentle breeze on my face clears my head a little. I take a deep breath and look up at the towering Buddha—set against a backdrop of green, leafy treetops and bright-blue sky.

"Before we went inside the statue, I didn't notice the seams between the different plates," I say to Adam. "Now I see every one of them. I can't ignore them. But I think they make the statue even more beautiful."

Adam gives me a small smile, and then he looks away.

* * *

At the admission booth for Hase Temple, I sheepishly place a still-damp bill—one that Adam and I rinsed at the money-washing shrine—on the counter in front of the attendant. I wish I knew how to explain in Japanese why my money is moist. The attendant's expression remains unchanged as he lifts the limp bill and replaces it with an admission ticket, my change, and an English map of Hase Temple.

"The Great Buddha was cool," Adam says halfheartedly as we stroll through the temple grounds.

"That Buddha used to be located inside of a building rather than out in the open, but the building was destroyed in a horrible storm," I say. "People rebuilt the building only to see it destroyed in another storm. They rebuilt again and the building was destroyed by a tsunami. After that, they decided not to rebuild. I guess the hall wasn't meant to be."

"If you believe in fate," Adam says. And he doesn't.

We duck under a bright-red torii gate and enter a small cave. I feel as if I've been instantly transported seaside, even though the seaside is miles away. The air is thick with humidity, and I can almost hear ocean waves crashing against a rocky shore. In the flickering candlelight, statues carved into the rock almost appear to be live people who could leap toward us at any moment. Water drizzles down the walls, like blood oozing from deeply abraded skin.

"What's the deal with this cave?" Adam asks,

examining the statues.

"It's dedicated to a sea goddess."

Adam leans in for a closer look at the face of one of the more intimidating carvings. "Is this her?"

"I'm not sure."

In one wall there is a tunnel, about waist high. A neatly-dressed Japanese woman wearing a skirt ducks down and enters the tunnel. An older woman follows her. Above the entrance to the tunnel There's a wooden plaque with four Kanji characters printed on it; I wonder if the letters explain what's ahead or merely say something along the lines of "Watch your head."

I'm eager to move on, and so I ask Adam, "Want to go in there?"

"Of course I do."

For an instant, I see the carefree Adam who I remember from what seems like ages ago. I can't help grinning at him. "You first."

The room on the other side of the tunnel is very small; it's more of a tunnel than a room. Off to the side is an even smaller tunnel, only about thigh high.

Adam gestures to the little tunnel. "After you."

I bend down and assess the narrow, dimly-lit space. If I were claustrophobic, I would not be able to enter this tunnel, but I'm not claustrophobic, not exactly. For a while—after Barry—being in small places bothered me, but only when there were other people in them with me. It wasn't so much being in a small space that upset me, it was the possibility that people would brush up against me. It was human touch that I was afraid of, not confinement.

I move into the tunnel. The roof is not high enough for me to stand and so I stay crouched low. Along the sides of the room—blanketing flat shelves of rock—are hundreds of tiny white statues; each one is about two inches tall and, as far as I can tell, indistinguishable from the next. I glance back to the cave entrance and feel a pang of anxiety, like something terrible is about to happen.

And then it does.

A wave of water suddenly splashes into the tunnel, obliterating the entrance. It swallows the shelves of statues. Tiny glimmers of the little white statues swirl inside the water as it heads toward me. In a moment, I'll be underwater. I take a deep breath and close my eyes, bracing for the water's impact.

But when the water hits me, it feels nothing like I'd expected. It embraces me, covering me with soothing warmth. I don't fight it. I don't want to. I'm safe here under the water. *I can still breathe.* I take a breath just to prove it to myself. And then I open my eyes.

Adam is facing me.

There's no water. There never was.

Adam looks at me with a mix of curiosity and concern. "What were you thinking about just now?"

"Drowning."

I'm not sure why I was thinking about drowning, and why I experienced the thought so vividly—like a nightmare that somehow overtook me even though I was completely awake. I can't help feeling that the experience was *given to* me by someone or something. The sea goddess? No, that doesn't make sense. But then, many things in my life don't make sense.

I turn away from Adam's furrowed face and move deeper and deeper into the cave, until I reach the end. I stare at the dead-end ahead of me, imagining myself tunneling into the Earth, far away from this world. My breaths come too fast. My heart pounds so hard that I feel as if it will give out. My head feels light and empty.

Adam comes up beside me. He doesn't say anything, but his hand finds my hand and takes hold of it, squeezing it tightly, as if he'll never let go. And we stay there, staring at the end of the cave, hand in hand, until I don't want to tunnel away from the world anymore.

Chapter Nine

Tonight I let Adam take the first shower—because he looked completely exhausted. When I enter the bedroom after my own shower, I'm surprised to find him sitting up in bed reading his book.

"I thought you'd be asleep by now," I say softly.

"Me too," Adam says, balancing his book on the tiny nightstand.

Before I can stop myself I ask, "Mind if we sleep together tonight?"

Adam lifts his covers and I slide under them, next to him. He pulls me against him so hard that it almost hurts, and yet I don't want him to let go.

Adam's chest rises and falls. I try to match my breaths to his. At first, it's difficult because his breaths are irregular and unpredictable, but the harder I try to find the rhythm of his breathing, the slower and steadier his breaths become. And then we breathe in perfect synchrony. I focus on our breathing, but instead of making me calm, with each breath my tension builds, as if a balloon is slowly expanding in my chest, about to explode.

Our faces move closer and closer together, as if we are pulled by an invisible force. I close my eyes and feel his lips just barely touch mine. And then our faces separate.

We didn't kiss. Not really. I'm not exactly sure *what* we just did. I stare into Adam's serious eyes, trying to ask him what's going on between us. I get the feeling he's trying to ask me the same thing.

"Should I go back to my bed?" I whisper.

"I wish you would stay," Adam says.

"Okay."

Adam pulls me to him. A few moments later, I feel him succumb to sleep. I exhale and let sleep take me too.

* * *

I awaken fully charged. Instantly, I become aware that my body is pressed against Adam's. I run my fingers lightly along the side of his ribcage.

"Good morning," Adam says through a yawn.

"Good morning," I say.

Adam tightens his arms around me. I close my eyes and take a pleasure-filled breath.

"Today we're leaving for Kyoto, right?" Adam asks.

"Right," I say.

"Guess we should get going."

I run my hand over Adam's silk nightshirt. We'll be spending the next three nights at a new hotel—in Kyoto. *I wonder if our new hotel will have Japanese nightshirts.* It makes me sad to think that it might not.

"We should probably do laundry before we check out," I say. "I don't think that our hotel in Kyoto has a laundry room."

"Good idea," Adam says. "And I need to make a phone call."

"Who do you need to call?" I ask, but then I realize the answer, before Adam even says it.

"Natsumi."

* * *

Right now it is yesterday evening in New York. I've tried not to think about what time it is in New York ever since I set my watch to Tokyo time when we took off from JFK airport. But now, as I listen to the washing machine swish my clothes together with Adam's, I can't help thinking about back home.

Adam is upstairs in our hotel room talking to Natsumi. He's probably comforting her, telling her not to worry because he will always be there when the baby needs him, and if she needs him as well. That's one of the things I admire about Adam, his loyalty. Still, it hurts. I press my palms against the washing machine lid and close my eyes, letting the coolness of the metal and the gentle vibrations soothe me and the sound massage my brain.

Something touches my shoulder. I spin around, ready to fight.

"Sorry I startled you," Adam says.

My hands fall to my sides. "It's okay. I was just … meditating. How was your phone call?"

"She didn't answer. I left a message," he says. "After that I went to check my email. I got another message from Michelle. She said that Natsumi is mad at her because she told me about the baby."

"Why doesn't Natsumi want you to know?"

"Michelle said that Natsumi said she didn't want to ruin my life too."

But what about the baby? Has Natsumi considered that her child will want to know his or her father?

I've traveled halfway across the world in an attempt to fill the void that my mother's absence left in me. Did my mother know that she would hurt me so deeply? If she did, why didn't that stop her?

* * *

The two-and-a-half-hour bullet train ride from Tokyo to Kyoto is supposed to be scenic. There's a poster at the front of our train car that shows majestic, snow-capped Mount Fuji with a bullet train in the foreground. On the poster, the sky is bright blue and cloudless. The photo must have been taken on a day very unlike today. It has been raining nonstop ever since we left Tokyo. Outside the train windows, all but our immediate surroundings disappear into the mist. Even so, I look out the window hopefully.

In the reflection in the window, I see Adam drop a bookmark into his book. He tilts his head back, looking up at the ceiling, and then he leans toward me. His chest lightly touches my back as he looks out the window.

Raindrops race across the outside of the glass, trying to distract me from Adam's reflection, but I find his eyes despite them. His eyes look into mine as the sun pokes through the clouds and the mist clears.

And then the city of Kyoto comes into view.

* * *

Our hotel room in Kyoto is much bigger than the one in Tokyo. And the windows are translucent rather than opaque. There isn't much to see through the windows though—just a bunch of geometric, non-descript buildings—but I can't help but smile when I see a sign attached to the building directly across from us that says simply, "Welcome!" in English. We are three stories up and the sign is at eye level, and so it must be meant for hotel guests. We're the only people who can see it.

"Which bed do you want?" Adam asks me, tossing his backpack onto a chair.

"I don't care." *I wonder if we'll sleep together in the same bed again tonight.*

Adam collapses onto the second bed.

I go to the other bed and notice neatly-folded, white, silk Japanese pajamas. I feel a surge of happiness. "They have Japanese pajamas!"

"Cool," Adam says—for my benefit I'm sure. "We could put them on right now if you want."

"Why?" I ask. "Are you tired?"

"No."

"Then why would we put on the pajamas?"

Adam just looks at me. *Is he hinting at what I think he's hinting at?* My heart pounds as if it is trying to break out of my chest.

"We haven't done our aimless wandering yet today," I blurt out.

"Why don't we go wander around and find someplace really nice to have dinner?" he suggests.

"But if we're looking for a place to eat, then we won't be aimless in our wandering."

Adam smiles. "It'll be aimless enough for me."

"Okay," I say absently, my mind still occupied by the pounding in my chest.

Adam goes to his suitcase. He opens it and tosses some nice pants and a button-up shirt on his bed.

"You know, I'm starting to like our aimless wandering," I say as I unzip my suitcase. The freshly-laundered dress I bought in Harajuku is right on top. I take it out and lay it on my bed. "Maybe we could wander aimlessly for a while and *then* find someplace for dinner."

"Deal."

Adam pulls off his t-shirt. I turn away. I don't want to see him undressed. If I do, I'll want to get close to him. I slip off my clothes and quickly pull my dress over my head. When I turn back toward Adam, he is buttoning his shirt.

"You look really nice," he says.

"So do you," I say, and then I catch a glimpse of myself in the mirror across the room. "My hair's a mess."

"It looks good."

I grin and shake my head at him. "I'm going to go brush it."

He shrugs. "Suit yourself."

I walk to the bathroom, close the door, and pick up my hairbrush. Suddenly, without warning, hot tears pool in my eyes. I grab one of the folded washcloths from the stack of clean towels, dampen it with cold water, and press it to my face, not exactly sure why I'm crying. And then I realize: *I love Adam. I love him so much.*

And that thought absolutely terrifies me.

Chapter Ten

Kyoto is a historic city with over 2,000 temples and shrines. While Adam and I are wandering aimlessly, we catch enticing glimpses of them peeking out over their surrounding walls: the sloped roof of a pagoda, a metal sculpture of a bird perched at the tip of a spire with its wings spread. The shops and restaurants near the temples and shrines—which I imagine were bustling with tourists just a few hours ago—are shuttered for the evening. It feels as if we're walking through an ancient Japanese ghost town.

The sky is beginning to darken as we turn down a narrow alleyway to head off to look for a restaurant. Adam glances down each street we pass, sometimes stopping to take a photo of a street sign or doorway. He's clearly in his element. That's one of the things I like most about our wanderings. I love watching Adam explore the world so optimistically, like it has something special to offer.

To our right is a fence. Adam goes to it and stays long enough that I decide to join him. On the other side of the fence is a small grassy park with numerous neatly-arranged towers of polished stone blocks. A concrete path circles the center, with worn dirt trails leading to each tower.

"A cemetery," Adam says.

"When I die, I want to be cremated and have my ashes scattered into the wind. Then anyone who cares about me can feel like my spirit is always with them."

Adam glances at me sideways. "You're not planning on dying anytime soon are you?"

"No," I say, and then I admit, "but I've been thinking about death a lot lately."

"What do you mean?"

"In Nikko, when we were standing on the bridge, I imagined myself jumping off and falling into the river below. And in the cave at Hase Temple, I imagined a wave crashing through the entrance and swallowing me." Adam doesn't say anything, and so I continue, "After Barry ... took advantage of me, I imagined myself dying a lot. I thought it was because I *wanted* to die. When I stopped wanting to die, I stopped having those thoughts." I haven't told Adam about these "death fantasies" before because, by the time I met him, they were history.

"Do you want to die now?" Adam asks quietly.

"No, I don't," I say, feeling certain.

Adam turns toward me. "You can tell me the truth."

I look into Adam's eyes. "That *is* the truth. I want to live. I've never wanted to live more in my whole life."

Suddenly, the whole universe disappears, except for Adam. I want to close my eyes and feel his lips press onto mine. I imagine his hand moving over my cheek and along my neck. I imagine my arms sliding across his back. I imagine his body pressing against me, so close that I feel his heart throb.

"Let's go find some dinner," Adam suggests.

"Okay," I say.

Adam leans against the fence again, looking out over the cemetery for a moment, then he starts back down the alleyway. After he takes a few steps, he turns around. "Coming?"

"Yeah," I say, and I follow him away from the cemetery.

* * *

Blurry streaks of yellow, white, blue, and red light shine in the lightly-rippled river that runs under the bridge that we cross. The sky is dark blue—almost black—and this reflected light, along with the light emanating from the windows of the surrounding buildings and streetlamps, is the only illumination in the darkness.

Lining the river's edge are the elevated wooden decks of restaurants. One of them has red lanterns strung across it. Imagining myself sitting on that deck with Adam makes me feel warm all over.

"Let's eat there," I say, pointing to the lantern-lit deck.

Adam looks at me, his eyebrows raised. "You haven't seen the menu."

"It doesn't matter what's on the menu. I'll just sit and sip tea if I have to."

Adam smiles. "I'm sure it won't come to that."

* * *

Being on the restaurant deck feels just like I imagined it would. I kneel on a flat cushion before a low table. Adam sits cross-legged on the other side of the table. The red lanterns give Adam's face a soft glow.

The waitress places small ceramic cups in front of us. She pours water into each cup and then sets the carafe in the center of the table.

"*Arigato*," Adam says to her.

She bows and leaves us.

I take a large gulp from my cup. Bitter burning warmth fills my mouth and spills into my throat. It travels through my chest until it disappears in my stomach.

"That's not water!" I say to Adam, swallowing again.

"It's sake," Adam says. "Sorry, I should have warned you." Adam drinks from his own cup and then says, "It's good."

I take another sip of my sake. I like the warm feeling of the liquid in my mouth and throat, but I wish it were sweet.

"So what do you think of Japan so far?" I ask Adam.

He takes a deep breath, as if he's inhaling the entire experience. "It feels different than I thought it would."

"Different how?"

His eyes ignite with passion. "The streets and alleyways feel vibrant and alive. The city feels like it's humming with restrained energy. And the temples and shrines feel peaceful and thoughtful." He looks away, as if he's embarrassed. "That sounds weird."

"No, you're right. Before we came here, I looked at so many guidebooks and websites that I thought I knew what it would be like to be here. But it's not like what I expected."

Adam looks into my eyes. "I'm glad I came here with you."

Maybe it's in response to what Adam just said, or maybe it's the sake, but I suddenly feel bolder than I should.

"Are you … attracted to me?" I ask him.

Adam looks down into his sake. "Yes."

Warmth radiates through me. "And you like me, right?"

Adam looks at me. "I love you, Erin."

My breath catches in my chest. "You mean you love me … as a friend?"

"I love you as a friend. And as a person. I just love

you."

The air around me suddenly feels warm, as if I am surrounded by that love. With Adam, I feel safe. With Adam, I feel certain. I swallow hard and say, "Then maybe we should be ... more than friends."

Adam's expression becomes very serious. "We can't, Erin."

My body suddenly loses all sensation. I feel numb. "Why not?" I speak with barely a sound.

Adam looks at me as if his heart is breaking.

I continue softly, "Whatever the answer is, it's okay. I just need to understand."

"The night that you told me about what Barry did to you ...You said you'll never be able to truly trust a man ever again. That it will always be in the back of your mind that he'll hurt you." Adam inhales as if the air burns his lungs. "Knowing you'll never be able to trust me ..."

"That's the reason?" My voice is barely a whisper.

"Yeah."

"The *only* reason?"

"It's a pretty big thing for me, Erin," Adam says.

Tears form in my eyes. "When I said that, I thought it was true. I thought I was too broken to ever recover my ability to trust anyone, especially a man. But I trust *you* so completely, more completely than I ever trusted anyone on Earth. Being with you feels ... right."

Adam looks like he can breathe easily again. "It

does."

"Like it was meant to be," I tease.

He smiles through glassy eyes. "I don't believe in fate."

"Yeah, well, I do."

* * *

Adam and I drank all of the sake. Adam drank most of it, but I'm definitely feeling the effects of my share as we stroll through an outdoor shopping mall that is closing up for the night. A few people wander around. A shopkeeper drags a display of bagged snacks into a store and then pulls the chain gate down over the entryway.

Adam smiles at me. I wish I could hold his hand, but I restrain myself. In Japan, public displays of affection are generally avoided, and so our touches must be stealthy. I let my arm brush against his and an electric tingle shivers through me. I wonder what will happen when we get back to the hotel.

Four giggling college-age girls pop out from behind a colorful curtain hanging from a large machine at the entrance to an arcade. The girls go to the side of the machine and collect some papers that the machine spits at them. They laugh and squeal at their prize and then stumble off down the street.

I approach the machine curiously and pull back one of the curtains. "A photo booth. Let's do it!"

Adam looks inside the booth. "How does it work?"

I'm not thinking that far ahead. "We'll figure it out."

"All right. Why not?" Adam goes to the side of the machine. He drops coins into a slot and the screen lights up with the number "2."

"Booth two!" I bounce over to the curtain labeled "2."

Another group of excited girls prances up to the machine and they drop in some money.

I close the curtain behind Adam. We are finally alone.

"Thanks for doing this," I say. "I know it's kind of girly."

"That's okay. I'm secure in my masculinity."

"You should be."

I lean toward him and close my eyes. Adam's lips meet mine, hungrily and passionately.

FLASH. The inside of the photo booth lights up.

"Did you push the start button?" I ask him.

"I guess so." Adam kisses me. His lips are warm and gentle.

FLASH.

"We should … look at the camera … for some of them." I say, between kisses.

"Okay." Adam turns toward the camera.

FLASH.

"Let's do some crazy poses," I suggest.

"Okay."

FLASH.

"How are you posing?" I ask.

"You'll see."

FLASH.

I smile at the camera, feeling happier than I've felt in a long time.

FLASH.

The screen changes. There are instructions there in Japanese.

"I think it's done," Adam says.

"Let's go see our pictures."

I pull back the curtain. Adam follows me to the side of the machine. There are no photos there.

We wait.

The group of girls who arrived after us join us, and the machine spits out their photos.

I turn to the girls. "Where are our photos?" I point to their photos, point to Adam and myself, and then hold up my hands as if I'm perplexed.

One of the girls gestures for us to follow her, and we walk back toward the photo booths. The girl draws one of the curtains. Instead of a photo booth, there are two computer screens inside. Our photos are posted on the screens, along with a clock ticking down the seconds.

"*Arigato gozaimasu*," Adam and I say to the girl.

We enter the booth and study the screens. They display a Photoshop-like program, but of course, the instructions are in Japanese. The clock ticks down: 2:42. 2:41. 2:40.

Adam and I each man a screen. After a few seconds of experimentation, I discover that I can drag different images onto our photos: hearts, animal ears, hats, stars, phrases. Some phrases are in English and some are in Japanese. I quickly set to work dragging and dropping until the clock reaches zero, and our photos disappear from the screens.

We go back to the side of the machine. This time, our photo strips are waiting for us. There are two strips: one that I decorated—I remember the zebra ears that I added to myself—and one that Adam decorated. On the first photo, we both added the same phrase: "True love."

Chapter Eleven

Adam and I stare at each other, full of anticipation. I wish the hotel elevator would move faster. I groan when it comes to a stop on the second floor.

The doors open and a Japanese woman wearing a business suit enters.

"*Konbanwa*. Good evening," she says as she pushes the button for the floor above ours.

"*Konbanwa*," Adam and I say.

"That's a pretty dress," she says to me, with hardly any appreciable accent at all. Then she gives a reserved giggle. "It's nice what it says."

I look down at the Kanji letters printed on my dress, intrigued. "What does it say?"

"'I have found my best friend, my lover, my soulmate,'" she reads.

I stare at the dress, feeling my eyes mist at the thought that the words there might be a sign that what is happening with Adam, what is about to happen, is meant to be.

When the elevator stops and the doors open, Adam touches my arm, awakening me from my thoughts. I follow him into the corridor.

"Have a good night," the woman says to us.

"You too," Adam replies.

"Goodnight," I add.

And then Adam and I walk to our room without saying another word; there are no more words that need to be said. As soon as our hotel room door closes behind us, I unbutton Adam's shirt, revealing his muscled chest. Adam lifts my dress over my head. I slip my fingers under his waistband to free the tucked edges of his shirt, as Adam attempts to unhook my bra. It takes him a few tries, even though he's using both hands. I stare at my reflection in the entryway mirror. I rarely look at myself undressed because my eyes are so critical, seeking out every imperfection. But now, what I see is beautiful. It is as if I'm looking through Adam's eyes.

"Let's take a shower together," I suggest.

Adam kisses me so softly that it makes my whole body ache. "Okay."

In the bathroom, I slip off my panties, turn on the shower, and step under the warm water. It flows over my hair and down my back. I close my eyes, appreciating the sensual experience.

And then Adam joins me.

He squeezes some soap onto his hands and rubs them together, then he places his fingers on my shoulders and begins to wash me.

"When did you fall in love with me?" I ask.

"Do you remember the day we took the train down to Washington, D.C.?"

"Of course I do." One weekend, when Natsumi was busy studying for exams, Adam and I decided on a whim to take a day trip. Spending that day with Adam is one of my favorite memories.

"We visited incredible museums and monuments, but the best part was that I was with you. That's how I knew I loved you. You outshined some of the coolest things in the nation." Adam spins me around and begins to work on my back. His fingers move down my spine, massaging the soap into my skin. "The next weekend, when Natsumi told me she'd found someone else, I accepted it instantly. Because I wanted to be with someone else too."

"I fell in love with you on the night my dad died," I say. "That's when I discovered that I could trust you wholly and completely. I climbed into bed with you, and all you wanted to do was comfort me. You didn't try to seduce me. You didn't try to take anything from me. You were just there for me. But I didn't allow myself to consider that we could be more than friends, because you had a girlfriend."

Adam turns me toward him. "But when Natsumi and I broke up, why didn't you …?"

"I figured eventually you would make your move. But you never did."

"Because I didn't think you could ever trust me."

"But I do … in every way." I lift his hands to my chest.

Adam silently washes my chest and then his hands spill onto my hips. I put my arms around him and pull him to me. Our bodies slide against each other, slippery with soap. I reach between his legs, and he closes his eyes and inhales. It seems strange to touch him like this. But it also seems right.

I look into Adam's eyes as his fingers slip between my legs and enter me. I forget everything except how much I want to be with him. My thoughts blur as he pushes deeper, slowly massaging my insides until they are tense with pleasure. And then, Adam releases into my hand. In that same instant, something explodes within me. I feel like I'm going to collapse, but Adam's arm around me keeps me upright. My lips rest on his until our shaky breaths slow back to normal.

And then Adam soaps up his hands. And he starts washing me again: first my neck, then my shoulders, and my arms, and my back, then my chest, and my belly, and between my legs, and from my thighs down to my feet. His touch feels different than before. Instead of feeling exciting, it feels comforting.

It feels like love.

* * *

I wake before Adam does. My naked body is half on top of his. His breathing is quick. *He must be dreaming.* I lie still, so I don't wake him.

Finally, Adam stirs. As the paralysis of sleep lifts, he moves his hand along my side, as if he's blindly exploring the world with his sense of touch. My skin tingles with energy.

"Good morning," he yawns.

"Good morning," I say. "What were you dreaming about?"

"You."

I skim his abdomen with my fingers and notice that his body is excited. "What were we doing?"

"We were wandering around Tokyo."

"And that got you excited?"

His cheeks flush. "I usually wake up with a …"

"Even when you're in bed alone?"

"Yeah."

"What do you do about it?"

"Nothing usually. It just goes away."

"Do you want to *make it* go away?"

Adam gives a small smile. "How?"

"Do you have protection?" I ask.

"Why would I bring protection? I didn't think …"

I didn't think we would be doing this either.

110

"Wait." Adam jumps up and goes to his suitcase. He pulls out a small gold paper bag sealed with a smiley face sticker.

"What's in there?" I ask.

"I bought it in Harajuku. It was a going to be a gag gift for my roommate." Adam unseals the bag and shows me what's inside: a small rectangular box sealed in plastic, with words on it in both English and Japanese.

"Condoms?"

Adam's cheeks flush. "He has a weird sense of humor."

I stare into Adam's eyes. "Do you think he'd mind if one was missing?"

Adam smiles. "I'm sure he'd understand."

"Let's brush our teeth first," I breathe.

Adam follows me into the bathroom. I grab my toothbrush and he grabs his. I've never brushed my teeth in front of a guy before. I try to be neat about it. Adam looks at me in the mirror and smiles. I laugh and some white foam escapes from my lips. I quickly wipe it away with my finger.

Adam says something, his voice muffled by a mouthful of toothpaste.

"What?" I ask, but it sounds more like "Uh?"

Adam brushes faster and then spits into the sink. He rinses his mouth. "I said, 'I never thought toothbrushing could be so arousing.'"

I lean into the sink, spit out my toothpaste, and rinse. Then I kiss Adam, slowly and deeply. We caress each other's bodies, until I ache for him. Adam takes my hand and leads me back to the bedroom. He sits on the bed and opens the box of condoms. I watch as he unrolls one of them onto himself. And then he's ready. We're ready.

Adam lies down. I take a breath and climb on top of him. My heart pounds furiously as, little by little, I let Adam enter me, filling me with heat. Our bodies move together in perfect rhythm. I'd thought this would feel awkward, but strangely, it doesn't.

As I kiss his parted lips, Adam releases inside me. An instant later, waves of warm energy overtake me, briefly pulling me into another universe before letting me go. And then I collapse into Adam's arms and breathe, as if I haven't breathed in years.

Chapter Twelve

Outside the entrance to Kiyomizu Temple, there's a place called Tainai-meguri. Or at least there is supposed to be. I don't see it, but that might be because I don't know what it looks like or even what it *is* exactly. It's on my mom's bucket list, but she didn't include much information. She merely wrote: "Experience Tainai-meguri."

There were no photos of Tainai-meguri in any of my guidebooks. Instead there were vague, intriguing descriptions. According to one guidebook, "Visiting Tainai-meguri is like symbolically entering the womb of a divine being." Another offered, "There's a rock in the darkness. Spin it and make a wish."

"What are we looking for?" Adam asks me.

"Possibly the most unusual experience in Kyoto."

Adam's eyes light up. "Awesome!"

We head up a stone staircase. At the next level of the

complex, most people are taking pictures of a three-story pagoda, but my gaze immediately goes to a queue snaking from the entrance of a plain brown and white building. All of the signs on the building are in Japanese, except one that says, "No picture."

"That has to be it!" I rush to the queue and take my place behind some boys who look like they might be in junior high school. Adam joins the queue behind me.

The boys in front of us step forward, take off their shoes, and place them into plastic bags handed to them by the attendant at the entrance. The man hands me a matching bag. I slide off my sneakers—still dingy from our muddy hike in Kamakura—and drop them into the bag.

In front of us is a staircase. The handrail is a rope of wooden beads, each about the size of my fist. I take hold of the rope and descend. My socks slip on the smooth wood of the stairs. The rope gives a little when I lean on it. Nothing feels very secure.

At the bottom of the stairs, the rope passes under a curtain. I glance back at Adam, and then I move into the darkness. I focus on the beaded rope in my hand. It feels as if it undulates as my fingers move over it. It calms me.

In the dark, there are usually shadows or shapes. Here, I see nothing but inky blackness so thick I can almost feel it. It's as if my eyes are shut in the dark of night even though they are wide open. There's no sound—not even footsteps. I think of Adam, following me without seeing me. I wonder how far behind he is. I wonder how far away I am from the boy in front of me. It seems unlikely that we are able to maintain a proper distance between us without our sense of sight or touch, but we've been walking for at least a minute now and I haven't felt the presence of anyone else. I feel entirely alone.

And then I see a faint light. People mill about in a small, barelylit room up ahead. Some of them have their hands on the edge of a rock the size of a big rig tire that lies flat atop a somewhat-smaller rock. Noiselessly, they turn the top rock, as if it's a huge record on an oversized old-fashioned record player. It is strange to watch; a rock that big shouldn't rotate so easily.

I search for Adam and find him searching for me. He touches my hand lightly, but he doesn't speak. No one here is speaking. Together, Adam and I go to the rock and take hold of it. I don't need to make any effort at all to spin it; it turns from the work of so many other hands, as if it's turning on its own.

"Make a wish," I mouth to Adam.

I close my eyes and make my own wish: *I wish that Adam and I will be together forever.* When I open my eyes, I see Adam open his. We release the rock and follow a stream of light to a curtain that leads to a staircase that takes us back to where we came from.

As we walk away from Tainai-meguri, Adam asks me, "What's the deal with that place?"

"It symbolizes entering the womb of a divine being," I say.

"Oh." Adam's tone is subdued.

"What did you think of it?" I ask.

"It made me feel uncertain, and yet completely certain." He looks into my eyes. "What did you think of it?"

"It felt … comforting." And then I realize how strange that is. Not long ago, the darkness—the unknown—absolutely terrified me.

For some reason, the unknown doesn't scare me so much anymore.

* * *

"Stand on the huge wooden balcony of Kiyomizu Temple and look out over the city of Kyoto" is on my mom's list. It is the first thing we do when we enter the temple grounds.

I walk to the balcony railing and look down at the distant ground below. "Long ago, people used to jump from this balcony," I tell Adam. "They believed that, if they survived the fall, they would get their wish." Given the distance, I'm not sure how *anyone* survived the fall, but I read in my guidebooks that some people did.

Adam looks into my eyes as if he is trying to read them. "Are you thinking about jumping?"

"No." Surprisingly—unlike when I stood on the bridge in Nikko—I'm not picturing myself plummeting to my death.

In the area below the balcony, I spot three skinny streams of water flowing out from under a grey rock roof and arcing into a pool. People reach out with ladles, collecting the water as it falls. One man holds his ladle to his mouth and drinks.

"That must be the sacred water," I say. "'*Kiyomizu*' means pure water. There's water here that grants wishes and brings you health if you drink it. My mom wanted to drink the wish-granting water. It's on her list."

Before we leave the balcony, I take one last look straight down. *Still no horrible images of death. Weird.*

* * *

Adam and I descend a long staircase that leads to the three streams and join the queue of tourists waiting to collect some sacred water. I watch tourist after tourist step up onto the platform behind the streams, grab a silver cup with a long metal handle attached, reach out and collect water from one of the three streams, rinse one hand with the water, fill the same hand with water, and then take a drink.

When it's our turn, we each pull a ladle from the row of metal bins marked "sterilizer," and we approach the water together. My arms are so short that, even when I hold the very end of the handle, I have to lean forward to reach the nearest stream with my cup.

I think of my mom. I imagine her standing here, reaching forward with the ladle, exactly how I am doing right now. My palms grow sweaty. My brain feels weak. My foot slips. I fall forward.

A strong hand grabs my arm and yanks me back before I plunge into the shallow, turbulent pool where the three streams come to an end. Adam pulls me to him. "You okay?"

My heart pounds. My hands shake. I feel dazed. "I didn't get any water."

Adam looks at his wet shirt. "I did."

I force a smile. "You're supposed to *drink* it."

He half-smiles back, not quite masking his concern. "Yes, I know."

I take a breath. "I need to try again."

"Are you sure?"

"It's on my mom's list."

With Adam's hand, holding my arm, I reach forward and collect a ladleful of water from one of the skinny streams. This time, the stream doesn't seem nearly as far away. I rinse my still-trembling hand and then fill it with water. And I drink. The water tastes clean. It cools my mouth and my lips. I take another handful and drink again. I feel as if the water makes me stronger.

Adam collects his water easily, with one hand. He rinses the opposite hand and then pours himself a handful of water. He drinks it, clearly enjoying the experience. He takes a second handful and drinks.

When he turns toward me, his lips are wet. I want to

kiss them. I wonder if it's wrong to have thoughts like that here; this is a sacred place.

I slide my ladle back into the sterilizer and walk down the steps on shaky legs.

"Do you want to sit down?" Adam asks.

"No," I say, "it's probably better if I keep walking."

And so we do.

It isn't until we've walked all the way to the outskirts of the temple grounds that I fully appreciate their beauty. The most impressive viewpoint is from the hillside opposite the balcony that we stood on when we first arrived. From here, I see that the balconied building is nestled, along with a collection of smaller buildings and a multi-tiered pagoda, on a hill alive with bright, leafy trees. Under the balcony, a network of thick wooden beams creates a lattice that disappears into the foliage below it. Adam puts his arm around me, his fingers resting at my waist. His wet shirt feels cold against the back of my arm. And then I realize we're alone.

"What happened back there at the sacred water?" Adam asks, interrupting my thoughts.

I stare into the distance. "I'm not sure."

"It looked like you spaced out or something—the same way you did in the cave in Kamakura." Adam takes a breath.

I swallow. "I was thinking about my mom. I felt like she was there with me. Inside my body."

Adam's forehead wrinkles into the same expression that people used to give me when I had my panic episodes—after Barry. I hate that expression.

I try to explain, "I guess I was trying to imagine what she might think or feel here."

Before Adam can respond, two Japanese girls—about eleven or twelve years old—wearing pressed navy-blue dresses over collared shirts, come giggling around the corner. As Adam takes his arm from around me, the taller girl whispers something to the smaller girl.

The smaller girl approaches us. "Excuse me," she says to me. "Do you speak English?"

"Yes," I say.

The girls share a nervous glance. The smaller girl continues, "Would you help us … with a school project?"

"Sure," I say.

"Thank you." The smaller girl opens her pamphlet. Staring hard at the words printed on one of the pages, she says very deliberately, "Where are you from?" Then she looks up at me expectantly.

"New York," I say.

The girls' eyes widen. "New York!" they say in unison. Then they scribble something into their pamphlets.

The taller girl finally speaks alone, "Where have you visited in Japan?"

"Tokyo and Kyoto."

"What is your favorite thing about Japan?" the smaller

girl asks.

That's easy. "The people in Japan are very nice."

The girls smile and then avert their gaze shyly.

"Why did you come to Japan?" the taller girl asks me.

"To find my mother." And, suddenly, I realize something: I didn't come to Japan just to follow my mom's bucket list. I was hoping to *find her.* Up until a moment ago, I didn't dare say it or even think it. But that is the truth. Tears form in my eyes; I blink them away before the girls finish scribbling in their pamphlets.

"Can we take a picture with you?" the smaller girl says, her gaze fixed on her pamphlet.

I force myself to smile even though my face is numb. "Sure."

The taller girl pulls out a cellphone.

"I'll take it," Adam offers.

The girls stand on either side of me and each raise two fingers in a peace-sign gesture. Adam snaps a photo and hands back the phone.

"Thank you very much," the girls say, and then they hurry off.

I lean against the railing and gaze out into the distance again. My vision is blurry. My heart pounds in my throat. "I came to Japan to find my mom," I say to Adam.

"You mean figuratively, right?"

I shake my head as hot tears roll down my cheeks. I wipe them away, but new ones instantly take their place.

Adam touches my shoulder. "Even if your mom is in Japan, the chances of you finding her are infinitesimally small."

I pull away from him, determination rising within me. "But it is *possible*. I know it isn't likely, but there is a chance." I turn away from the railing and start walking.

* * *

I'm really not in the mood for this, but I climb the stone staircase—decorated with signs sporting garish black and red Kanji letters—that leads to Kyoto Jishu Shrine. A small plaque beside the stairs says, in English, "Here is the Famous LOVE STONE."

At the top of the stairs—at either end of a small courtyard lined with wooden booths—are two more-or-less-identical, boulder-sized "love stones." It is said that, if you are able to walk from one stone to the other with your eyes closed, you will find true love. I had been excited about giving this a try, but now, my heart just isn't into it.

Adam reads the English-version of the sign by the first stone and then asks me, "Are you going to do it?"

I shrug. "It's on my mom's list."

I put my heels against the first love stone and look straight across the courtyard, at the matching stone. There are no obstacles in my path, except the people who are wandering about. *This should be easy. I just need to walk straight.* I close my eyes and the world becomes red-pink—

the color of my eyelids when sunlight shines through them. I take small shuffling steps, keeping my hands out in front of me; I don't want to walk into anyone.

Around me I hear the murmurs of tourists having conversations that I can't understand. They grow louder or softer as I move toward or away from their sources. The people who are speaking might be moving as well. It's hard to tell.

Strangely, I haven't bumped into anyone yet. Walking through a crowd of distracted people with my eyes closed, I should have accidentally brushed against at least one of them by now. I wonder if people in Japan are more careful about avoiding knocking into others than people back home. I don't recall accidentally brushing into anyone since I arrived in Japan, even in the busy train stations at rush hour.

Suddenly, my hands hit something solid: wood. But there was nothing wooden anywhere near the second love stone. I must have veered off to the side of the courtyard, into one of the booths. My eyelids begin to throb; if I were to open my eyes, tears would start to flow. *I failed.* I turn away from the obstacle and shuffle ahead with my eyes closed, uncertain how long I should keep going before I give up. And then my foot hits something solid. Applause and cheers break out around me. I open my eyes and see Adam standing in front of me. My toes are pressed up against the love stone at the far end of the courtyard. I made it!

"How did I get here?" I ask Adam.

"You peeked," Adam says, as if the answer is obvious.

"No." *I didn't.*

"After you started walking, I went off to the side to take pictures. And you followed me. Then, I went over behind the stone and you turned around and came straight to it. Tell me you did that without looking."

"I did." *But how?* "When I started walking, I was positive that I was going straight. But instead of heading to the stone, I went ..." My eyes widen as I realize: "I went toward *you*. I only went to the stone when *you* were behind it. Maybe it was bringing us together."

"You probably heard me walking or snapping pictures," Adam offers.

Tears pool in my eyes. "Why does there always have to be a logical explanation?"

He sighs. "Because there always is."

My happiness tears away from me so quickly that I feel the pain of the emptiness it leaves behind. "I need to believe that sometimes things happen that defy logic. If I don't, how can I ever hope to find my mom?"

I'm glad that Adam doesn't answer me. Because I know what he would say if he did: "You can't."

Chapter Thirteen

Adam and I haven't spoken since we left Jishu Shrine. Over the past hour, using a map from one of my guidebooks, I navigated our way on foot and by train to our next destination: Arashiyama. The journey gave me something to focus on besides all of the thoughts swimming through my head.

We cross a low footbridge over a deep-green river lined with verdant hills. Narrow boats with makeshift roofs, piloted by men with long poles, ply the water. On the other side of the river is Arashiyama Monkey Park, a place where guests can feed wild monkeys. Visiting Arashiyama Monkey Park is one of the few things I planned to do in Japan that weren't on my mom's bucket list. I wanted to come here for Adam.

Adam and I have gone to the Central Park Zoo many times. Each time, we spend at least an hour watching the

Japanese snow monkeys. Adam told me that he finds primates incredibly fascinating because they're so much like us. I thought Adam would enjoy getting up-close with them.

At the end of the bridge is a hand-painted sign depicting a cartoon monkey tossing a cookie into his mouth and pointing to the right. And so we turn right. The next monkey sign is not far away; it has an arrow that points toward the mountain. A set of worn stairs brings us to the monkey park's admission booth.

Adam reads the English words on the booth's sign and then turns to me, with hesitant excitement. "There are monkeys here?"

"Wild ones."

"Cool!"

We pay our admission and start along a path that winds up the mountainside. Tall trees form a canopy high above us. I scan the treetops, searching for monkeys, but about twenty minutes into our walk, I still haven't seen any. I haven't seen any other humans either.

The trail ends in a clearing at the top of the mountain, where the sky is big and blue and the city of Kyoto looks like a lake—made of miniature buildings—that laps at the bases of tree-covered mountains.

And then I see at least a half-dozen grey, shaggy monkeys with bright-pink faces just hanging out at the top of the mountain. There are no fences or screens separating us from them. Most of the monkeys are lazily lounging by a rock-lined pond. One monkey dips his hands into the water, as if he's washing them, and then begins to methodically examine another monkey's fur.

"This is amazing!" Adam breathes.

A man in a khaki uniform directs Adam and me toward a wooden shack that has wire fencing over its glassless windows. A monkey sits regally on the roof. A few monkeys scale the windows. On the dirt next to the shack is a very tiny monkey—about half the size of a human newborn. His mother is nearby, keeping us in her sights as if we are a potential threat.

The baby strays, possibly a little too far, and the mother grabs him by the leg. Her long arm lifts the baby and places him on her chest. She deftly climbs up the shack walls to the wire windows, stretches her arm through an opening, and snatches a peanut presented to her from inside the shack by a little boy. The boy turns to the woman with him and says something in Japanese, grinning.

The man in khaki slides open the glass door to the shack, allowing Adam and me to enter, and then shuts the door tightly behind us. The inside of the shack vaguely resembles an old-fashioned schoolroom, with a schoolteacher-like woman at a large desk and rows of wooden benches filling the room. On the woman's desk are plastic sandwich bags filled with peanuts and apple slices. There is a small sign that says, "100 yen."

I trade a 100-yen coin for a bag of apple slices and go to the window that the little boy is leaving. The mother monkey is waiting there, her arm stretched through the fence. As I approach her, she looks directly into my eyes. Her fingers open, ready to accept what I have to offer. I hold out a slice of apple. The pads of her fingers gently touch mine for a split second as she takes it. She puts the food into her mouth and then swings her hand back to me. I give her another apple slice.

Adam joins me with a bag of peanuts. The monkey stretches her hand toward him and he passes her one. She opens the peanut shell with her teeth and empties the nuts into her mouth, letting the bits of shell fall onto the infant who suckles peacefully at her chest. His eyes are closed, as if he's asleep, but his small mouth moves in short bursts.

Suddenly, the baby opens his eyes—instantly alert. He looks at me.

"Hi, little guy," I can't help saying.

I pull out my camera to snap a picture. As I aim, I feel a tap on my hand.

I look at Adam. "What?"

He laughs. "It wasn't me." He nods toward the mother monkey, who is holding her hand out to me. "I think she wants more apple."

I give her an apple slice. As soon as she deposits it in her mouth, she taps Adam's hand.

I grin. "Now she wants a peanut."

Adam passes her a peanut and turns to me. "I'm glad this was on your mom's list."

I decide not to tell him the truth.

* * *

When we finally leave the feeding shack, Adam and I have spent about 1,000 yen between us on apple slices and peanuts.

We follow a narrow trail leading toward the tip of the mountain. There are more monkeys here than there were at the feeding shack. A few are sprawled out—like monkey rugs—with other monkeys picking through their shaggy fur. Some sit in tree branches, munching leaves. I focus on a female perched on a thick branch just a few feet away. She stares at nothing in particular as she chews on a twig that still supports a few green leaves.

I look down at the corrugated metal roof of the feeding shack and the little pond next to it, reflecting the sky in its glassy surface. Monkeys dot the landscape; they are as ubiquitous here as squirrels are back home in New York. I feel a pinch of sadness in my gut.

When I was a little girl, I used to sit on the porch in my parents' backyard and watch squirrels collect nuts and chase each other up and down our big oak tree. One time, while I was sitting out there, my dad walked through the dining room. I heard the wooden floor creak with his footsteps, but I didn't bother turning around. I stayed still, trying to make myself as invisible as I felt.

"What are you doing?" my dad asked through the screen door.

"Watching the squirrels," I mumbled. My dad never took much of an interest in what I was doing, and so I figured he was about to scold me because I'd disturbed him in some way. Maybe I'd accidentally left the light on in the bathroom or he was upset that I'd left the back door open because it was starting to get cold outside.

He came out onto the porch, sat down next to me, and said, "I used to watch the squirrels when I was a kid."

And then we went on to have an actual father-daughter conversation. I don't remember what was said exactly. I'm pretty sure we talked mostly about squirrels, but *what* we talked about didn't matter. What mattered was that—for those few moments—I felt like he liked me. From then on, every time I would sit and watch the squirrels, I would think back to that time on the porch with my dad and I'd smile—even though we never had a conversation like that again.

When my dad died, the bank sold our house; my dad owed more on it than it was worth, and I couldn't afford the huge payments that would have been required to keep it. The new owners tore the house down and built two houses on the land. They knocked down the oak tree too.

Adam gently puts his arm around me, as if he read my thoughts.

"Everything and everyone I ever loved is gone," I whisper to him, "except for you."

He reaches up and strokes my hair. "I promise I'll love you forever."

I shake my head. "Nothing lasts forever."

"Souls do. And that's where I love you, in my soul. I always will."

And at that moment, I realize that, even though Adam doesn't believe in fate, and even though he probably never will, Adam and I were meant to be.

* * *

I enter our hotel room alone. Adam stopped at the business center to check his email. It will probably be at least a few minutes before he gets back to the room. I slip off my sweaty, dusty clothes and look at my naked body in the long mirror in the entry hallway. I still like what I see.

I turn on the shower and step into the warm spray. I squeeze some soap from the dispenser and rub it over my face, neck, and chest, remembering Adam's hands massaging soap over my slippery skin, and the tingle of pleasure I felt wherever he touched me.

A door slams. *Adam must be back.* I hurry to finish my shower.

When I enter the bedroom, Adam is sitting on the end of his bed, staring at the wall. "I got another email from Michelle." He takes a long breath. "Natsumi is in the hospital. She started having contractions."

This isn't good. Natsumi is only six months pregnant. If she were to have her baby now, the baby would be extremely premature.

Adam continues, "My mom had premature labor twice when she was pregnant with me. I was finally born three days *late*." He sounds hopeful, but he looks worried.

I sit next to him and fold him into my arms.

* * *

The room is dark. Something's ringing. The phone.

I lift the receiver. "Hello?"

"This is Aki," a young male voice says as if it's a question rather than a statement. "Is Adam there?" Even though he's speaking English, it takes me a moment to process what he said. Aki is Natsumi's brother. He stayed with Adam for a few days back in the fall when he was visiting colleges in New York City. I never met him.

"Hold on," I say. I reach over and gently shake Adam's shoulder. "Aki's on the phone for you."

Adam rubs his eyes, still half-asleep. "What?"

"Aki's on the phone," I repeat.

Adam instantly becomes alert and takes the receiver. "Aki, it's Adam." Adam doesn't speak again for a long time. Finally he says, his voice faltering, "Okay, bye." Adam hangs up the phone and lies back down next to me.

"It's a boy," Adam whispers.

I put my arms around him and hold him, as tightly as I can.

Chapter Fourteen

Adam takes a deep, forced breath—the kind of breath people take when they're trying to keep it together.

"The baby is really sick," Adam says. "The doctors aren't sure if he'll make it."

"Do you want to fly home early so you can be with him?" I ask.

"Aki said that Natsumi doesn't want me there. Her family wants me to respect her wishes."

Adam hugs me as if he's trying to squeeze out sadness from deep inside his body—sadness that is too deep to budge. Then he releases me, climbs out of bed, and opens the sliding panels that cover the windows. Morning sunlight floods the room.

"Today we're going to go to Nara, right?" Adam asks, opening his suitcase and taking out some clothes.

"We don't have to do anything today," I say. "We can stay here at the hotel if you want."

He shakes his head. "I want today to be normal."

But it can't be normal.

Adam continues quietly, "Let's just do what your mom planned."

"All right."

* * *

I spend most of the hour-long train ride from Kyoto to Nara unsuccessfully attempting to nap. I open my eyes as the train pulls into Nara station. I watch Adam slip his book into his backpack and then I stumble out of the train after him. I'm already starting to feel the fog of sleep deprivation.

My mom had two things in Nara on her bucket list: "Attain enlightenment by crawling through the tunnel in the column behind the Great Buddha" and "Feed the deer at Nara park." Nara Park is famous for the friendly deer that surround its historic sights. The Japanese believe that deer are sacred, and so the animals are allowed to roam freely. Because tourists are encouraged to feed the deer—shops sell "deer crackers" for that purpose—they've become socialized with people.

Just inside Nara Park, we see our first deer. It's strange to see a deer so close. The ones I saw on a camping trip in Upstate New York ran away before I got much of a look at them; all I saw of those deer were the white undersides of their stubby tails as they darted away. This deer approaches us. She has sand-colored markings on her golden-brown fur. I hold out my palm to her—the way I would for a friendly dog. She considers it and then turns and walks away. She finds a spot in a cluster of sleepy deer lounging near the roots of a tree and lies down. None of the other deer acknowledge us.

Nearby, an ancient-looking woman with a worn face and loose clothing sits on a crate that might have once held bottles of soda. Beside her is a plastic cooler. A handwritten note taped to the side says "150" and the symbol for yen along with some Kanji letters. She leans forward, her hands on her knees, and points to her cooler. "Food … for deer."

Adam pulls out some coins and holds up two fingers. "*Ni.*"

The woman's knobby hands take the coins and then fumble with the latch on her cooler. Adam moves forward to help her, but she waves him away with a small bow. She finally eases the cooler open and hands Adam two stacks of crackers—that look like wafer-thin silver dollar pancakes—tied with a paper cord. Adam hands me one stack.

Deer move toward us from different directions—mostly female deer, but a few male deer with threatening-looking antlers. Soon we are surrounded. Four of them circle Adam and five engulf me. I pull the paper tie from my crackers and stuff it into my pocket. The old woman watches us with smiling eyes.

The crackers look too big for the deer's small mouths. I break one cracker into fourths and hand off the pieces to the deer that beg for my attention, while simultaneously avoiding the antlers that move toward me as the male deer lower their heads to take their crackers. *This is more intimidating than fun.*

Adam works his way to me as he feeds a crowd of deer that pursue him as if he's a pied piper. Soon he's standing next to me.

"I'm out," Adam says of his deer crackers. "How do you still have any left?"

I pass him two crackers. "I've been breaking them into pieces." I snap my last two crackers into quarters and continue feeding my crowd of deer.

"They're very enthusiastic," Adam says.

"Yeah, it's a little scary." I give my final cracker piece to a large male, and then I hold up my empty hands, showing them to the animals. "Sorry, guys. That's it." One deer takes a bit of my shirt in her mouth. I pull it away from her and wave my hands in the air. "No more."

The deer finally back off. I grab my camera and take some photos of the few that remain, with a moss-covered stone lantern—like the ones we saw in Nikko—in the background. Then we follow the gravel path deeper into the park.

We turn a bend and see a lone deer ahead of us. She approaches us and then stops next to me, letting me stroke her side.

"I wish I had some crackers for you," I say to her.

Adam unzips his backpack and puts a few crackers in my hand.

"I thought you ran out," I say.

"I bought another stack while you were taking pictures. I figured it might come in handy."

The deer raises her head, but then she just stands there. It seems unlikely—given my last deer-feeding experience—that she's waiting patiently for me to offer her a cracker. *Maybe she's not hungry.* I break one of the crackers and hold out a piece for her. "Do you want this?" The deer gently takes the cracker piece that I offer. And then she dips her head down and brings it back up again.

"What's she doing?" I ask Adam, even though he's no expert in deer behavior.

Adam offers her a piece of cracker. She takes it and dips her head again, keeping one eye on us.

Adam smiles. "I think she's *bowing!*"

I give her another piece of cracker. The deer lowers her head again, twice in a row, and then raises her head expectantly.

"I think you're right!" I say.

Adam takes out his camera. "I'm going to get some video."

I give the deer another piece of cracker and bow. She bows. I bow back to her and give her another cracker piece.

She bows again.

"Got it!" Adam says.

"Let's get a picture of the three of us," I suggest.

"Okay." Adam stands next to the deer and aims his camera as we pose. "One, two, OWW!" He snaps a photo.

"What happened?" I ask as the deer walks off.

He rubs his bottom. "She bit me!"

"On your butt?" I stifle a giggle.

"It isn't funny," he says with a half-laugh.

"It kind-of is," I say, trying to surpress my smile.

Adam checks the picture on his camera. And then he starts laughing so hard that tears roll out of his eyes. He holds the camera toward me so I can see the picture. On the screen, Adam's face is crinkled in an expression of pure agony.

I laugh, but feel empathetic. "Did she bite you hard?"

"I'm sure she left a mark."

Without thinking, I touch the small wet spot where Adam's shorts entered the deer's mouth. Our gaze meets, and then it locks. A fire grows between us, comforting … and irresistible. I want to kiss him—a kiss that erases all pain. I imagine his lips on mine. Breathing him in. Our bodies pressed together. Feeling warm and whole and full.

I lean toward him, letting my eyelids fall.

* * *

Past a sprawling pond—where the deer relaxing along the

grassy banks are as plentiful as the ducks—is a flower-lined path leading to a huge building with a tiled roof that turns upward at each corner. It reminds me of buildings we've seen at other temples, except this one looks like it belongs to a giant rather than mere humans.

We enter the building through doors that could accommodate a person many times our height. Ahead of us is an enormous Buddha statue made of dull metal. The Buddha is flanked by two somewhat-smaller statues and sits before a backdrop that makes it appear to be sitting on a throne. Decorations adorn its base: candles atop gold candlesticks, gold pots set on pedestals, and fan-shaped plaques lined with painted flames that almost appear to be real fire.

According to the guidebooks, this Buddha is bigger than the one we went inside in Kamakura, but to me it looks smaller, probably because the soaring ceiling above us dwarfs it. I wonder if this is what it was like to visit the Great Buddha of Kamakura before its temple hall was washed away.

I circle the Buddha, distracted by the geometry of the beams overhead. Thick, wooden columns stretch from the ceiling to the floor, supporting the massive building. In one of these columns is the tunnel that my mom wanted to crawl through. I might not have noticed the tunnel if it wasn't for the queue of schoolchildren extending away from it.

"There's a line for the 'enlightenment tunnel,'" I say to Adam.

"I'm sure it's worth the wait," Adam says, joining the queue.

One at a time, each of the kids ahead of us squirms through the tunnel as other children laugh and call out to them—maybe goading or teasing. Once the last child has passed through the column, Adam slips inside. The tunnel is taller than it is wide, and so he lies on his side, his hands stretched above his head. I watch his body, then his legs, and finally his feet disappear into the tunnel. After a few moments, he wriggles out the other side. He pokes his head around the column to smile back at me.

"You made it!" I say to him.

"Yup, no problem!"

My head feels dizzy as I approach the tunnel entrance. Ignoring my pounding heart, I squat down, lift my arms above my head, and slide on my right side into the tunnel.

Inches in front of my face is smooth, dark wood; it is all that I see. I can't tilt my head up enough to look ahead or down enough to see behind me. I try to pull myself forward, but there's nothing to grasp onto. I attempt to propel myself with my feet, but I can't gain any traction. I am stuck.

Suddenly, I hear a piercing scream. A woman's scream. It seems to be coming from inside the tunnel, but it can't be; I'm not screaming, and the tunnel is too small to accommodate anyone else. The sound fills my head, like a nightmare. My heart pounds. My breaths come fast. I struggle for air, but find none.

"Help!" My yell sounds like a whisper.

The scream grows more intense. The sound stabs my eardrums like jagged needles. I wish I could plug my ears with my fingers, but my arms are stuck high above my head.

My hands reach out, searching for something to grasp onto. There is nothing. I try to push myself forward with my toes. My sneakers slip. The screaming grows louder. Agony erases every thought in my head … except one. Although I don't remember ever hearing my mom scream, I feel like it is her scream that I hear now.

"Stop screaming … *Please* …" I plead.

Suddenly, the screaming ceases. It's quiet except for my rapid breathing.

I find a bit of tenuous traction behind me and inch my body forward. My fingernails discover tiny grooves in the floor. I claw myself along.

First my elbows pass the threshold. And then my shoulders. I crawl ahead on my forearms and spill out of the tunnel, empty and exhausted.

Adam offers his hand to help me to my feet, but I shake my head. "You all right?" he asks.

"While I was in the tunnel, did you hear someone screaming?" I ask.

Adam's forehead furrows. "No."

That's what I thought.

* * *

When we get back to our hotel, Adam and I go to the business center so he can check his email for news about the baby. I sit at the computer next to him and sign into my email. After I finish deleting all the junk, I look over and see that Adam is just staring at his computer, his expression blank.

"Aki sent me a video of the baby," he says, without taking his gaze off the screen.

"Did you watch it?" I ask.

He shakes his head. "I can't."

"Do you want me to watch it with you?" I ask.

I don't want to watch this video; I don't want to see Adam's baby struggling to survive, but Adam nods. And so I roll my chair close to him and watch the little white arrow click the big red arrow over the frozen, blurred image of a skinny baby.

The video comes to life. The tiny chest—whose ribs are visible through the nearly-transparent skin—begins to move unnaturally; a machine is breathing for the baby. The baby's legs lie lifelessly on top of a pink-and-blue-striped blanket. Both of his arms are strapped down to little boards. A syringe hangs off a tube that protrudes from the baby's belly button. The camera moves in on the baby's face. His cheeks are practically covered with thick white tape that wraps around a tube emerging from his gaping mouth. His eyes are closed.

And then the video ends.

* * *

Adam and I walk back to our room in silence. Adam removes his shoes, goes to his bed, and lies down. And then he cries harder than I've ever seen another person cry. I climb into his bed and hold him. I hurt for him. I'd take all of his pain for myself if I could—so he wouldn't have to feel it. I'm used to pain. When I get too much, I get numb, but being numb is bearable. I don't think Adam knows how to make himself go numb.

I brush my lips against his—lightly, softly. He opens his wet eyes. I kiss them closed and run my fingers over his forehead, feeling it relax under my touch. He breathes me in, seeming to draw strength from me, yet taking nothing. I go back to his mouth, letting my lips meet his again. This time he kisses me back. Hesitantly. Then more certain. I lift his t-shirt and kiss his chest. His heart pounds beneath my lips.

I will take away his pain, if only for a few minutes. I go to his suitcase and find the box with two little packets left inside. I grab one and return to Adam. Without a word, I lower his shorts and boxers, open the packet, and unroll what's inside onto him. I slide off my shorts and panties, and I push him into me. He moans and pushes back. I kiss him again, parting my lips. He gently rolls me onto my back and plunges deep inside me.

In a flash, I see ... hear ... smell ... feel *Barry.* My heart pounds in my throat.

It's Adam, I tell myself. *I'm here with Adam.* But in my mind, I can't escape Barry. Fear builds inside me, taking the place of the oxygen in my lungs.

Hard push. I don't feel it. My body is numb. But not my brain. I wish my brain were numb too. *Why can't I make my brain go numb?* Push. *Stop!* Push. *Stop it!* Push. *Please ... please ... stop.* Tears fall silently down the sides of my face.

He moans and releases into me.

And then it's over.

Adam's heavy eyes open. They focus on my face and then instantly fill with concern. "Did I hurt you?"

I'm breathing so fast that my fingers are tingling. "No, you didn't hurt me."

Adam strokes my hair. "What's wrong then?"

I hold my breath, trying to stop myself from losing it. *Adam is probably blaming himself for upsetting me. I can't let him do that.* I exhale and suck in another breath. "When you were on top ... it reminded me of Barry."

Pain washes over Adam's face. "Erin, I'm so sorry." He puts his arms around me, but I pull out of his embrace. I can't stand to have anyone hold me right now. Not even

Adam.

"You didn't do anything wrong," I say, crawling to my feet. "It's not your fault I'm messed up."

Adam grabs my arm. "You are *not* messed up."

I look into Adam's eyes. There is no judgment there.

"Let me go," I say so softly that I'm not sure if I'm speaking it or thinking it.

Adam releases his grip. I turn away from him and walk to the bathroom, my heart aching. *Adam was hurting. I tried to help him. But I made it worse.*

I run to the bathroom and turn on the shower. Without waiting for the water to warm, I step under the spray and let cold water hit my deadened skin.

Chapter Fifteen

Blinding white morning sunlight pours into our room. We must have forgotten to close the sliding panels over the windows last night.

Adam is already awake. He's not reading or anything. He's just staring at the TV screen. And the TV is off.

"Morning," he says.

I'm glad he didn't say, "*Good* Morning." Because it doesn't feel good.

"Morning," I say.

"When's our train to Hakone?"

We'll be spending today and tonight in Hakone. Tomorrow morning, we head back to Tokyo. Tomorrow night, we fly home to New York. I don't want to go home.

I glance at the clock. "In an hour and a half."

"We'd better get ready then," he says.

"Right."

Adam goes to his suitcase and starts pulling out some

clothes. I head to the bathroom to wash up.

I'm glad we have a train to catch. That forces us to keep moving. I need to keep moving.

* * *

We begin our exploration of Hakone in a verdant valley surrounded by tree-covered hills topped with puffy gray clouds above sprawling Lake Ashi. There's a fake pirate ship docked here that looks like it would be more at home at Disneyland than in the real world. The next thing on our itinerary is boarding one of these ships to travel across the lake.

I turn to Adam. "Want to do some aimless wandering here?" I ask softly.

He gives a muted smile. "Do you even need to ask?"

I felt like I did.

We walk along the shore of Lake Ashi. Past swan-shaped pedal boats plying the water. Past gray-haired ladies enjoying lunch at a lakeside picnic table. Past a group of elementary-school-aged kids who are fishing in the lake.

As we walk, I'm slowly infused with the light-headed sensation that I now recognize as my mom's presence. But, this time, I sense eager anticipation rather than the usual panic. My mom must have come this way, but to see what? Whatever it was, it wasn't on her bucket list.

A small rock staircase leads us into a pine forest. Being in the forest reminds me of the nature walks I took with my mom when I was little. My mom liked to watch the birds and squirrels and tell me make-believe stories about them. One time we saw a squirrel jumping from tree to tree. She dubbed him "Sam." She told me that Sam was searching for the tallest tree in the forest so he could call out to his love and she would hear him. It was a silly story, but it was my favorite because, when Sam made it to the highest treetop, he actually started vocalizing. And then another squirrel seemed to come out of nowhere. She leapt over to him and chased him down the tree, and then up another one. That tree was where they would make their home and live happily ever after—or so my mom said.

"Look at that." Adam points to a huge red torii gate about fifty feet away from us, its base partially submerged in Lake Ashi. The bright color of the gate contrasts sharply with the muted greens and browns of the lake, trees, and sky. It looks both out of place and like it belongs.

A strange, happy glow comes over me.

"Can you take my picture with it?" I ask Adam.

He pulls out his camera, and I start down the narrow concrete path that leads to the torii gate, passes under it, and then disappears in the water. I continue walking until I'm standing directly below the gate. The lake laps against the sides of the path; I wonder if the water has ever risen enough to swallow it. I feel a little unsettled, like I might lose my balance. I turn back toward Adam and steady myself. Adam raises the camera. FLASH.

I start back toward him, but Adam raises his hand to stop me. He passes his camera to a man next to him and then walks to me.

As Adam poses under the gate with me, a stray breeze off the lake billows the bottom of my shirt, exposing my bare mid-section. Adam pulls my shirt back into place and rests his hand on my side. FLASH.

Adam retrieves his camera, and then we continue walking through the forest.

"I feel my mom here," I say quietly. "But it isn't like the other times. She isn't upset. She's happy. This is the first time I've felt her when she wasn't panicking."

My hair whips against Adam's face, but he doesn't move away. "Maybe you feel any of her strong emotions. Positive or negative."

I smile. "You're actually trying to make sense of this?"

"That's how my mind works."

A strong gust of wind hits my skin. I'm sure it's cold, but it feels warm, comforting. "But this doesn't make any sense at all."

"It could be some kind of sixth sense," Adam finally says.

I shake my head. "You don't believe in stuff like that."

He takes a deep breath. "Right before Aki called, I was having this dream. It wasn't like a normal dream. It felt incredibly vivid. It was about the baby. He was crying. It was a *he*, not a *she*. I was searching for him. Every time I thought I was getting close, the cries would get further away. I couldn't help him." Adam turns toward me. His eyes are wet.

* * *

The pirate ship that transported us across Lake Ashi docks at the foot of an aerial tramway. We follow the crowd ahead of us to a queue, where we wait to board one of the trams that travel up the mountain.

Once I get a look at the small trams, suspended from skinny cables, my palms begin to sweat and my feet tingle. This tram ride seemed like it would be fun when I imagined it. Now I wish there were another way for us to travel to our next destination. A way that wasn't so … confining.

I watch the family in front of us board a tram. The attendant closes the door behind them and the tram ascends. Then the attendant waves us forward. Adam climbs into the empty tram, and I force myself to follow. I sit next to him, in the back of the tram. A man and a woman—who look about the same age as Adam and me—take the seats at the front of the car, facing us. The woman clutches the bottom of her seat, her knuckles white. My gaze meets hers. I recognize the panic I see there; for an instant, I see my mom.

The attendant slams the tram door closed. I startle.

*I'm not afraid of this. This is **my mom's** fear.* I tell myself. *I can do this.*

I inhale. *One Mississippi, Two Mississippi, Three Mississippi.* Suddenly, the tram jerks. I gasp. The woman's fingers tighten on her seat. I look up and see that we just passed under one of the tram towers. *That explains the turbulence.* The woman follows my gaze and then sheepishly half-smiles at me. I half-smile back and slowly exhale. *Three Mississippi, Two Mississippi, One Mississippi.*

"What a view!" Adam says, looking through the window behind us.

I turn to see shimmering Lake Ashi blanketing the valley floor far below us. The pirate ship that took us across the lake is now heading back, its deck full of new passengers.

I pull out my camera and hold it out to the woman across the tram. "Can you take a picture of us?"

I'm not sure how to say that in Japanese, but she seems to understand. Her fingers release their grip on the seat to accept the camera.

After she snaps a photo, I whisper to Adam, "Crazy pose."

I widen my eyes and splay my fingers by my ears. I'm sure that Adam is doing something funny as well, because the woman's gaze moves between the two of us and she giggles as she takes another picture. I try to hold back a laugh, but a snort escapes through my nose. The man across from us, who had been politely ignoring our antics, starts laughing. And then Adam and I start laughing uncontrollably. The woman takes another photo, of us laughing. Then she hands back my camera. She smiles at me—a full smile this time. I full-smile back.

I settle back into my seat to take in the view. Outside the tram, clouds rise from the mountainside—like smoke without fire.

Slowly, my happy glow fades, leaving me feeling empty. And then I realize why.

I've discovered how to make my mom's fears go away. And that's good.

But I made my mom go away too.

* * *

The smoke rising from the mountainside turns out to be steam created by water entering deep fissures in the earth. We walk along a roped-off path through the eerie landscape of steam vents and shattered rocks stained white and orange. Apparently the area outside the ropes is quite dangerous—judging by the abundance of caution signs with warnings written in multiple languages.

At the end of the path, tourists stand at long wooden tables littered with eggshells that are black on the outside but white on the inside. They peel blackened eggshells from hardboiled eggs, and then sprinkle the eggs with salt and eat them. Nearby, a grey-uniformed man pulls a rack of black eggs from a boiling pool of milky-blue water, and then he plunges a rack of white eggs into the pool. The man brings the black eggs to the back of a small stand where people line up to buy them. I join the line.

"You want to eat an egg?" Adam asks me.

"Eating a 'black egg' is on my mom's list," I say. "The guidebooks say that eating one adds seven years to your life."

Adam grins. "Then I'm eating at least two."

We trade a 500-yen coin for a brown paper bag containing five black eggs. Then we sit with our bag on a boulder overlooking the steam-covered, bubbling pool and each pull out an egg.

"To seven extra years," Adam says, tapping his egg to mine.

"To seven extra years," I agree.

We knock our eggs against the boulder and peel away the black shells. Soon our eggs look like any other hardboiled eggs. Pure white. I take a bite that reveals the dark-yellow yolk inside. I'm not a big fan of hardboiled eggs, but this is the best one I've ever tasted, cooked to perfect firmness with only the slightest hint of egg flavor. Adam and I each devour two and a half eggs.

"That's seventeen-and-a-half extra years each," Adam says after swallowing his final bite. "What are you going to do with all that extra time?"

"Travel the world!" I say.

He studies me with mock suspicion and then smiles.

"What did you do with the real Erin Beatrice Winters?"

I inhale the lightly-sulfur-scented air and smile back. "I think I found her."

* * *

On our way back to the tram station, I spot a sign featuring an appetizing picture of a soft-serve ice cream cone. It isn't until we are standing at the ice cream counter, ready to place our order with the woman who works there, that we learn that there is only one flavor of ice cream available: *egg* flavor.

"Eww," I whisper to Adam. But curiosity overwhelms me. "I want to try it anyway."

We pass some yen to the woman at the counter. She swirls yellow-orange ice cream into two cones and hands one cone to Adam and the other to me.

I take a bit of ice cream into my mouth.

"Terrible?" Adam asks.

"Delicious!" I say. It tastes like yellow cake!

Adam gives his ice cream a taste. "Oh, that's good!"

We can't take our ice creams on the tram, and so we sit on a bench overlooking the parking lot to savor our surprisingly-yummy egg-flavored soft-serve.

"I figured out how to control my mom's fears," I say to Adam.

"How?"

"There's a breathing exercise I learned. After Barry.

For when I used to feel panicky. I tried doing it when we were on the tram. And it worked. The panic disappeared." I take some more of my ice cream into my mouth and let it slowly melt before I swallow it. "But when I control her fear, I don't get to sense her at all. I wish I could feel her happiness again. Like earlier today in the forest."

"Maybe you felt her happiness at other times and you just didn't realize it."

I think about the happy moments I've had on this trip. Shopping at the dress shop in Harajuku. Sipping sake at the restaurant with the red lanterns overlooking the river. Making crazy poses in the photo booth. I wonder if any of them belonged to my mom too.

"Mount Fuji!" Adam breathes.

I follow Adam's gaze to the clouds ahead of us where I see a faint image, like the cone of a volcano. But almost as quickly as it appeared, Mount Fuji's image fades. Tears pool in my eyes as I watch it disappear.

"Mount Fuji was on your mom's list, wasn't it?" Adam asks.

Mount Fuji *was* on my mom's bucket list. But Adam only saw her list once. A few months ago. And he didn't look at it long. "How did you remember that?"

"It was the only thing on there with a question mark," he says.

Mount Fuji is often hidden by clouds. I assume that my mom's question mark meant that she knew she might not be able to see it. I wonder if my mom saw Mount Fuji. I feel like she did.

Adam smiles. "Does that mean you've done everything now?"

"Almost."

* * *

There's just one thing left on my mom's Japan bucket list that I have not yet done, and it's the one thing that, I'm not looking forward to doing: bathing in one of Hakone's natural hot springs, called onsen. Bathing in a hot spring sounds pleasant enough, but in Japan, this type of bathing is done in the nude.

In an empty locker room that looks like a smaller version of the one at my high school, I take off every bit of my clothing and stuff it into a tiny locker. I grab the white, hand-towel-sized towel that I purchased at the reception desk—because I didn't know to bring a towel of my own—and head into a narrow hallway, trying not to think about the fact that I'm completely naked.

Adam isn't with me. At this onsen, like most onsens in modern Japan, bathers are segregated by gender. Adam and I had to separate at the entrance to the locker rooms. We agreed to meet back at our hotel room in an hour.

The hallway opens into a room with walls of dark wood. Along the perimeter of the room and down the center are low showerheads—at about chest level. Wooden stools are below each one. Naked Japanese women of various ages sit on some of the stools, washing themselves. There are no walls or curtains between the showerheads. There is no privacy at all.

Everyone is required to shower thoroughly before bathing in the hot springs. I've never taken a shower in front of anyone except Adam. To me, the process feels too intimate to share with strangers. But here I must.

I choose a stool as far as possible from the other bathers and start to wash myself. First my face. Then my hair. Then my back, chest, and belly. It's difficult to wash my bottom while I sit on the stool, and so I stand up, lather my hands, and self-consciously wash between my legs. I wash my thighs, and then I sit down again to wash my calves and feet. I rinse, but don't bother drying off because the air is warm and I'm about to get wet again.

Outside the bathhouse are numerous small pools connected by a winding stone path. Anxiety grows in my chest as I step into the sunlight, feeling fully exposed. I want to get into a pool as soon as possible. I want to hide my body in the water.

Most of the pools are packed with softly-chatting bathers, with no room for any more. I rush to the pool furthest from the bathhouse. It's nearly empty—there are just two women sitting on a rock in the center, near the entrance to a cave. As I hurriedly climb over the boulders lining the edge of the pool and into the water, I slip a little, accidentally splashing the women on the rock. My cheeks redden. I expect the women to glare at me, or at least glance over to see who disturbed them, but they don't.

The water is scalding hot, but I lower myself into it quickly, wishing I could completely disappear into it. I direct my gaze up to the sky because it's the only direction I can look and not see anyone else. I stare at a small streak of blue between some clouds. And I exhale.

The heat of the water penetrates my skin and seeps deep into my muscles. I feel as if the knots in my soul are being untwisted. I close my eyes, and my thoughts get fuzzy.

* * *

When I open my eyes, the women who were sitting on the rock are gone. Now that there are no naked people near the entrance to the cave, I allow myself to look at it. As I stare at the opening, a dizzy, tingling feeling spreads from my head to my body. *I feel my mom.*

I hadn't thought I'd sense her here. Although "bathe in an onsen" was on my mom's bucket list. She didn't name a particular onsen, and so I just chose one from the list in one of my guidebooks. The book didn't describe them at all or provide any photos, and so I selected this one pretty much randomly. It doesn't seem possible that I picked out the same onsen my mom did, but if I feel her presence, maybe she was once here.

I don't consider whether or not I *want* to go into the cave. I just start swimming toward it. As I approach the entrance, fear rises within me. It fills my throat like vomit. I can taste it. But I don't hesitate. I keep going forward. My body trembles. My heart pounds. I don't try to control these feelings; they are my mom's. I want to feel her one last time, even if it hurts.

The air inside the cave is thick with humidity, like a sauna. My heart beats so fast that I think it will give out. My breaths come quickly. I feel like there isn't enough oxygen here. But I force myself to keep swimming until I'm as deep within the cave as I can get.

When I look back toward the mouth of the cave, I feel an intense desire to escape. Instead, I drop to my knees on the cave floor, the water level at my neck, looking out at the small bit of the world I can see, feeling like I'm about to die.

And then the cave entrance contracts, swallowing me inside. Water rushes into the closed cave, filling it fast. I jump to my feet, but by the time I am standing, the water level is above my head. I swim to the surface, treading water and breathing the dwindling air between the water and the cave ceiling. The air pocket becomes smaller and smaller. I breathe desperately, my face pressed against the sharp rock of the roof of the cave. The rock cuts into my lips, making them bleed. I breathe until there is no more air to breathe, and I have no choice but to surrender.

That's it, I tell myself. *It's over.*

Slowly, I let my last breath out of my lungs and sink down into the water. Lower and lower. To the center of the cave. Where I float. Weightless. I spread my arms as if they are wings. As if I can fly. Suddenly, warm arms wrap around me—*my mother's arms*—snatching me from an imaginary sky. She brings me close to her, tenderly, the way she held me when I was very little.

"You're going to be okay, Erin," my mom says. "Just breathe."

But I'm submerged in water. If I breathe, my lungs will fill with fluid. I'll drown. I'll die. But I follow her instructions anyway. I close my eyes and I take a long … slow … deep breath.

With a roar, the cave entrance blasts open. Bits of rock fly in every direction. Stinging my skin. The water level inside the cave falls fast. And I fall along with it. Down to the floor of the cave where I sink down to my knees, the water level at my neck once more. The cave is silent, except for the soft dripping of water from the cave walls. Everything is exactly as it was before.

Except for me.

My heart beats quietly in my chest. My breaths are slow and steady.

For the first time in *exactly* fifteen years, even though I am all alone, on my own, I feel safe.

* * *

I slide open the door to my Hakone hotel room. Orange sunlight streams through the rice-paper window coverings, giving a golden hue to the tatami floor mats. I slip off my sandals and walk barefoot toward the two bed pads set out on the floor. Adam is sprawled out on one of them, wearing shorts and a t-shirt. His body is still flushed from the hot springs, like mine.

"How do you feel?" Adam asks me, without opening his eyes.

"Like Jell-O," I say, lying down on the pad next to him.

He laughs. "So you enjoyed the onsen then?"

"It was a strange experience, but I'm so glad I did it." Someday I'll tell Adam what happened in the cave, but not now. "How did *you* like it?"

"It was like being in a peaceful, quiet … guys' locker room."

I laugh and roll on my side, inhaling the scent of Adam's t-shirt. For an instant, I remember sitting on the couch in his dorm room, cuddled under a blanket together, our bodies not touching, but our souls connected. That blanket smelled like this shirt.

Our mouths come together. Lips. Then tongues. Lightly. Then hungrily. Passionately.

"Let's get naked," I say.

Adam laughs. "You haven't had enough of being

162

naked this evening?"

"No."

I sit up, pull my shirt over my head, and drop it beside me. I unhook my bra as well. Adam watches me, looking intrigued, and then sits up and slides off his shirt. We both pull off our shorts and underwear. And then we kneel, facing each other, staring into each other's eyes. Completely undressed.

Adam's body is excited, but his face is calm. I push him down onto his bed pad and straddle him. His hands come to rest on my hips. They are eager, but restrained.

"Touch me," I breathe.

"I *am* touching you."

"Touch me *however* you want to touch me."

Adam's hands rise up my ribs and over my chest. He explores my body with an intensity that makes me ache.

"I want to make love to you," I whisper.

Adam looks into my eyes, studying them. "Are you sure?"

"I've never been more sure of anything in my entire life."

Adam consents with his eyes. I kiss them closed and retrieve the last little plastic package from the box in Adam's suitcase. I tear it open and unroll the contents onto him. Then I pull him on top of me. And I surrender.

Warmth washes over my body as Adam slides inside me. We stare into each other's eyes until mine grow heavy with pleasure. Adam's lips find my lips, and then they lose focus. He presses his forehead to mine. Our breaths are shaky. Energy builds within me as we pull and push. I can't think anymore. I can only feel. I feel no fear. No pain. No numbness. I feel warm and safe. I feel every nerve in my body, and yet I can't tell anymore where I end and Adam begins. Until Adam explodes inside me. I feel him release into me again and again, even though the world is blurry and blinding because I am exploding too.

And then the world is dark and still.

Chapter Sixteen

Adam and I didn't eat breakfast this morning. We starved ourselves for the chance to eat our final breakfast in Japan at the park with the log fort—the same park where we ate our first breakfast in Japan. It was Adam's idea.

It's already late morning by the time we arrive in Shinjuku. On our way to the park, we stop at our old hotel to drop off our luggage. When we checked out a few days ago, the woman at the front desk offered to store our luggage on the day of our flight home, even though that flight wasn't until a few days later. She gave us a note to explain that we were recent hotel guests.

When we hand that note to the man at the front desk, he asks Adam, "You are Adam Harrington?"

"Yes," Adam says.

The man goes to a box on the wall behind the counter and retrieves a sealed envelope with the hotel logo in the corner. He hands it to Adam. "For you."

Adam opens the envelope and reads the note inside. Then he inhales, as if he is gathering strength. "I need to call Natsumi."

"Is everything okay?" I ask.

"I don't know."

* * *

I browse a rack of brochures from places in Japan that I will never visit. Every so often, I glance at the glass-enclosed phone booth where Adam is. His back is to me. He hung up the phone a few minutes ago. Now he's just sitting there with his forehead resting against his hand.

When he finally pushes the phone booth door open, his face is as ashen as it was on the morning he found out Natsumi was pregnant—maybe more so.

"How is Isamu?" I ask him.

"He's good," Adam says somberly. "Really good. He's not on the ventilator anymore. He's breathing on his own now."

"Then what's wrong?" I ask.

"Natsumi told me the real reason she broke up with me. There wasn't another guy. Not exactly." He swallows, as if what he's about to say hurts him to say it. "The week before she broke up with me, she'd found out she was pregnant. She was actually excited about her pregnancy. She didn't tell me about it over the phone, because she

166

wanted to give me the news in person. But two days before I came to visit, she was walking home from the library and a man grabbed her. He took her behind a building and forced himself on her."

His words sink into me. *Someone hurt her.*

Adam continues, "She was ashamed. She didn't think I would still want her …"

"*Would* you have still wanted her?" I ask quietly.

"Of course I would have."

"So if she'd told you the truth, you'd still be together?"

He inhales. "I'm pretty sure we would be."

"Do you *want* to be?" I ask. I'm not sure if I'm ready for the answer to that question, but if Adam wants to be with Natsumi, I will let him go. Even though I don't think I would be able to recover from the devastation of losing him, I will let him go. I love him too much not to.

"Do I want to be with Natsumi?" Adam asks, his brow furrowed.

I nod rather than speak, because I am certain that if I speak, my voice will break.

"I wish what happened to her never happened. I care about her very much," Adam says. "But I'm glad Natsumi and I broke up. Because I love *you*."

Adam wraps his arms around me and I rest my head against his chest, listening to his steady heartbeat. We stay like that for what feels like an eternity before we start off on the same route we walked on our first morning in Japan. This time, however, we know exactly where we're going.

* * *

Today, the park is not empty. A small Japanese boy and girl explore the log fort. Two middle-aged women chat nearby. We sit on the same bench where we sat days ago and eat our Family Mart spoils as we watch the two children play.

"Do you want kids?" Adam asks me.

We've never talked about that kind of thing before, but up until a few days ago, any plans I had for a future family didn't seem to have much to do with Adam. Now it seems like they might—or even will—involve him.

"Definitely," I say.

"How many?"

"Two or three. I didn't like being an only child. I always wished I had a brother or sister." I smile. "Are you thinking about our future together?"

Adam looks down shyly. "Is that bad?"

A grin spreads across my face. "No."

The women quietly collect the little boy and girl from the fort. I watch them until they are completely out of sight. Then I leap to my feet and race toward the fort. Adam passes me as we climb the ladders to the upper level.

When I get to the landing, Adam is waiting for me, fighting a mischievous smile. Without a word, he takes my hand and leads me into the tower. Once we are crammed inside its graffiti-covered walls, he grips my shoulders and guides me to him. His lips meet mine. His tongue caresses and then devours my lips so passionately that it consumes my thoughts and makes my body hot with desire. I finally have to pull away, because I need to catch my breath.

"Last time we were here … I wanted to do that … so bad," Adam says, breathing hard.

"Me too."

I kiss him again. Deeply. Fiercely.

But this time, I remember to breathe.

* * *

The only place in Japan that my friend Setsko insisted that Adam and I visit is a tiny restaurant that she said serves amazing okonomiyaki—a dish she described as "a savory pancake that doesn't really taste anything like an American pancake." And so we stroll the streets of Asakusa, following Setsko's hand-drawn map, looking for the little restaurant.

On a street lined with mom-and-pop shops, I'm enchanted by a window display featuring two human-sized rabbit mannequins standing in what looks like a spaceship. The rabbits remind me of the teddy bear mannequins we saw in Harajuku. One rabbit is pink and wears a flowery robe. The other is light blue and is wearing a brown, striped robe. The robes remind me of kimonos, but I assume, given the sign above them that says, "Try on yukata. Take photo free," that the rabbits are wearing yukata.

Adam follows my gaze and then cringes. "You want to go in there, don't you?"

"I *really* do," I say apologetically.

Adam shrugs and then smiles. "All right."

We go inside.

The shopkeeper—a middle-aged Japanese woman with her jet-black hair in pigtails—greets us. *"Irasshaimase."*

I nod to her and begin browsing the racks of flowery yukata.

The shopkeeper approaches Adam and gestures to the far corner of the store. "Man over there."

"I'm okay," Adam says.

"I show you," she persists.

"Okay." Adam follows her stiffly, as if he's walking to his doom.

Once the shopkeeper has Adam obediently looking through the men's yukata, she comes to me.

"You try on?" she asks me.

At that moment, my hand rests on a yukata with faint pink and purple hydrangea flowers, like the ones at the love shrine in Kamakura.

I smile. "This one."

The shopkeeper slips the yukata from the hanger and guides it onto one of my arms, around my back, and onto the other arm. She wraps it across my front and then finishes it off with a thick sash that covers most of my chest and belly. I turn and discover Adam behind me.

"You look … beautiful," he says.

"You try on too," the shopkeeper says, hustling Adam back to the men's corner of the store.

She leafs through the yukata, stopping occasionally to assess Adam's response. On her fourth try, she shows Adam a plain, dark-blue robe.

He gives a slight smile. "I'll try that one."

The shopkeeper dresses Adam and then presents him to me.

"You look really hot!" I whisper to him.

"You have camera?" the shopkeeper asks. "I take photo."

I pull out my camera and pass it to her. She snaps two photos, one horizontal and one vertical. Then she hands the camera back and begins to untie Adam's sash.

"*Ikura desu ka*?" Adam asks her for the price. He gestures to both of us.

"You think we should buy them?" I ask him.

He smiles. "Why not? My treat."

I look down at my elegant, silky yukata. "But when will we ever wear them?"

"Today," Adam says.

The shopkeeper writes something on a notepad—the price, I assume—and shows it to Adam.

Adam turns to me. "Come on. They're a steal."

"Okay," I say, feeling a surge of happiness.

Adam reaches under his yukata, pulls out a few bills, and lays them on the shopkeeper's plastic money tray.

"*Arigato gozaimasu*," she says, replacing the bills with his change.

A moment later, we step outside wearing our yukata. We are the only tourists around, and the only people wearing traditional Japanese clothes, but for the first time since I arrived in Japan, I feel like I belong.

* * *

At the location that Setsko triple-starred on her map, we find a squat shack that is dwarfed by the modern, nondescript office buildings surrounding it. The shack is covered in so much thick, green foliage that I wonder if one day it will completely disappear into the vegetation.

We open the wooden door and find ourselves in a tiny entryway. Ten low tables fill the adjacent dining room. Every table is occupied by families or couples, except for one in the far right corner that sits clean and bare. On the dark walls of the dining room are a hodgepodge of faded posters and homely handwritten signs. A fan in the center of the room circulates warm air filled with the enticing aroma of cooking meats and veggies.

An old, wrinkled Japanese woman wearing a weathered apron gestures to the shoe cubbies lining the floor of the entryway. We slip off our shoes and put them into adjacent cubbies. Then the woman leads us to the empty table. Once we are seated, cross-legged, on the flat cushions that lie on the tatami floor, she hands us menus, written entirely in Japanese.

I pull out my diet explanation card and hand it to her. "*Osusume wa nanidesu ka?*" I ask for a meal recommendation.

She points out two different items. I point to the first one. Adam points to the second one. The waitress leaves us for a moment and then returns with two batter-filled ceramic bowls and two plastic cups of ice water. She places one of each next to me and the others next to Adam, gestures to the dark metal griddle set into the center of our table, and says, "Pour batter. Wait five minute. Flip. Wait five minute. Ready."

I roll up the flowing sleeves of my yukata and pour the chunky liquid contents of my bowl onto the griddle, making a puddle. Adam pulls back his sleeves and pours his batter onto the griddle next to mine. Food that needs cooking usually doesn't look too appetizing until it's cooked and the okonomiyaki batter is no exception. As we watch it slowly become more appealing, Adam sips his ice water and stares at me. I sip my water and stare back at him.

Adam grins the grin I fell in love with before I allowed myself to fall in love with him. "I like being with you."

I inhale happiness. "I like being with you too."

"Time for flip," our waitress announces as she approaches our table.

She hands me two spatulas, and I use them to flip my okonomiyaki. When I pass the spatulas to Adam, I notice that our waitress is standing nearby with a somewhat-younger, slightly-less-wrinkled waitress. They are both watching us intently.

"*Kawaii*," the younger one says.

"What did she say?" I ask Adam.

"It sounded like '*kawaii*,' which means 'cute,'" he says, flipping his okonomiyaki. "It also could have been '*kowai*,' which means 'scary.'"

I laugh. "I'm hoping she said, 'Cute.'"

The younger waitress whispers something to our waitress.

"Beatrice," our waitress responds, looking at me.

My heart nearly stops. *I must have heard her wrong.*

"Did she say 'Beatrice'?" I ask Adam.

"Your middle name?" he responds.

"It's also my mom's *first* name." I turn to the women. *Could they possibly have met my mom?* "Beatrice … Winters?"

They look puzzled. *Of course they do. They don't know my mother.*

But then I have another thought. I try my mom's maiden name, "Beatrice Sands?"

The waitress' jaws slacken.

"They know her. They know my mom," I say in disbelief. "Adam, how do you say 'daughter' in Japanese?"

I ask him urgently.

Adam pulls out his Japanese dictionary, and I look up the word for daughter: "*musume.*"

I point to myself. "*Musume,*" I try.

"Food ready," our waitress says approaching our table again and laying out two plates.

She uses the spatula blades to swiftly chop each okonomiyaki into four pieces. She slides a piece of mine onto my plate and a piece of Adam's onto his. Then she sprinkles each piece with brown and white sauces. I see what she's doing only in my peripheral vision; I am staring at her face, urging her gaze back to mine. When she returns the spatulas to the table, she finally glances at me.

"I'm trying to find Beatrice Sands," I plead. "She's my mom. I haven't seen her in many years. Do you know where she is? Beatrice *doko desu ka*?"

"*Hai.*" She bows and leaves us.

My eyes fill with tears of frustration. "She doesn't understand what I'm asking," I say to Adam.

"We'll figure this out," he says, rapidly paging through his dictionary.

I look down at my food. It smells wonderful and looks delicious, but I'm not hungry anymore.

"Erin ..." Adam says.

When I look up, our waitress is standing next to me, holding a printout from a Japanese version of Google maps with two addresses marked.

She points to one address and says, "We are here." Then she points to the other address and says, "You walk. Ten minute."

I point to the second address. "Walk to what?"

"Beatrice." She hands me the printout, bows, and goes off to tend to a family at another table.

"'Beatrice' must mean something in Japanese, like hair salon or clothing store," I say to Adam. Still my heart pounds with hope. "Do you think there's *any* chance that this is my mom's address?"

"It's extremely unlikely," Adam says. "But we'll go there. And we'll find out." He looks at our food. "Do you want to eat first?"

"We probably should." I fold the map and slip it into my backpack. And then I take my first bite of okonomiyaki, my last meal before I—possibly—find my mother.

Chapter Seventeen

We've been walking for more than ten minutes. My legs shake with anticipation. I show the map given to us by our waitress to yet another pedestrian and ask, "*Doko desu ka*?"

The man points to an odd multistory building just half a block away that looks like a real-life version of something from a cartoon. It appears to have been constructed by precariously balancing a bunch of slanted-roofed, single-story houses on top of one another, creating the illusion that the structure might topple to the ground at any moment. *Could this be my mom's apartment building?*

My entire body trembles as I approach the doorway. There is a sign there—printed in Japanese and in English: "Asakusa Culture Tourist Information Center."

A lump forms in my throat. "The waitress sent us to a tourist center." Even though I knew deep down that the chances I would find my mom here were slim, my heart aches.

Adam's face looks pained. "There's probably someone in there who can write down your questions about your mom in Japanese, then we'll go back to the restaurant and—"

I shake my head. "No. The waitress doesn't know my mom. I just believed what I wanted to believe. You were right, there's no such thing as fate." Tears fall down my cheeks. "I'll never find my mom. It was ridiculous to try. I'm done." I sit down on a bench and try to make myself okay with that.

"Well, I'm not." Adam marches toward the open doors of the tourist information center.

I wipe away my tears with my fist and go after him.

By the time I catch up with Adam, he's already speaking with a uniformed woman behind the information counter, asking her—in Japanese—if she speaks English.

"*Sukoshi*," she answers. "How may I help you?"

"We're looking for someone," Adam says.

I take a breath. "What does 'Beatrice' mean in English?"

Her forehead wrinkles with confusion. "Beatrice … is American name."

I try a different approach. "We were at a restaurant. I asked, 'Beatrice *doko desu ka*?' And we were told to come here."

I put the map that the waitress gave us on the counter.

The woman's fingers move over some Kanji letters scribbled near the bottom of the page. I hadn't noticed them before.

I point to the letters that she touches. "What does that say?"

"You are daughter of Beatrice Sands?" she asks.

My body goes numb. "Yes," I breathe.

"Go to floor number seven." She points to an elevator bank. "Elevators there."

"*Arigato gozaimasu,*" I hear myself say.

* * *

Adam and I are alone in the elevator. His hand is in mine; I don't know when it got there. I stare at the inside of the elevator doors, unsure of what will happen when they open. *Will my mom be there? Will she be angry with me for finding her? Or will she tell me she's sorry that she missed seeing me grow up? What if she wants me to go away? Or stay here in Japan, with her?*

My body is trembling again. I fight to make it still. I don't want to be trembling when I meet my mom. I want her to see me as the adult that I sometimes feel like, not as the little girl that I feel like right now. I want her to be proud of me.

The elevator doors open on the seventh floor. A gentle breeze comes from the huge open balcony. A woman stands there, facing away from us. I know right away that she isn't my mom. Her skin is too olive and her hair too dark.

Opposite the balcony is a small café with no patrons.

"I guess I should ask someone who works here," I say to Adam.

"Do you want me to come with you?" he asks.

I squeeze Adam's hand hard enough that I can feel it through the numbness that has taken over my body, then I release it. "I need to do this alone."

As I walk to the café counter, I take a deep breath. It doesn't make me feel any calmer, but I doubt there's anything I can do to prepare myself for what's about to happen. I've been waiting for this moment almost my entire life.

A sandy-haired man sitting behind the register jumps to his feet as I approach. "*Konnichiwa*. What can I get for ya?"

My heart feels as if it will burst from my chest. "Is Beatrice Sands here?" I ask softly.

He shakes his head. "She hasn't worked here for a long time."

"But she *used to* work here?" I ask, incredulous.

"Yes."

She was here. "Where is she now?"

"I haven't seen her in over fourteen years."

My eyes burn. I got here fourteen years too late. Still, this is the closest I've ever been to finding my mom. I can't give up. "Is there anyone here who might know where she could be?"

The man's eyes narrow. "Are you ... Erin?"

"How do you know my name?" I ask slowly.

He smiles warmly. "Your mom talked about you all the time."

I feel a burst of pride. *My mom talked about me.* Based on his tone, she said nice things. "Were you friends with her?" I ask, the pain of hopelessness dampening my spirit.

"Ever since college."

I freeze as a horrible thought enters my mind: "Did she come to Japan *with you*?"

He looks down at the counter. "Yes."

Anger floods my body, filling my lungs. I can hardly breathe. "She left *her family* to be with *you*?"

"Erin, no, it wasn't like that," he says.

"What was it like then?" I ask, my jaw clenched to keep the words from becoming screams.

"Your mom was dying."

I don't believe him. "She wasn't dying."

"She had terminal brain cancer," he says quietly.

I shake my head. *That can't be true.* "How *dare* you say that? My mom did *not* have cancer. My dad would have told me."

"He didn't know."

My brain tries to grip what this man is saying, but it slips. I need proof, but he's offering none. "So she got cancer and she just ... went to Japan? Without me? Without my dad? Why would she do that?"

He looks into my eyes. "She didn't want her baby to watch her die."

And suddenly, I know he's telling the truth. In fact, I am absolutely certain of it. And then I realize why. As I stare, unblinking, into this man's eyes, I see my own eyes—the same brown-green eyes I've seen in the mirror my entire life. I always wondered where I got those eyes. My mom's eyes were bright blue, and my dad's were deep brown. This man's eyes are *exactly* like mine.

"Were you and my mother ever … together?" I ask in a voice that's barely audible.

He breaks our stare. "Once."

"When?"

"Your mother and father were going through a tough time and—"

I stop him. "How many years ago?"

"Nine months before you were born."

My dad was tall and thick. I am short and thin. My dad had sun-kissed skin, even when he didn't get any sun. My skin is pale. I just assumed that I look more like my mom than my dad; a lot of people look more like one parent than the other. But now, looking at this man, I see the missing pieces. The waves in my hair. The curves of my upper lip. The color of my eyes.

"You're my father," I say hesitantly—not because I'm uncertain of my conclusion, but because I am afraid of his reaction. I don't think I can take another parent abandoning me.

"You were very small when you were born. The doctor said you were a few weeks premature. That would have meant that your mom got pregnant after she and your father got back together." He fidgets uncomfortably, the same way I do when I'm upset. "If I'd thought you were my child, it would have been impossible for me to leave you."

"What do you think *now*?" I ask.

"You *are* my daughter. There's no doubt in my mind," he says. "Do you want to go for a walk?"

The air feels thick and heavy. "Can you give me a minute?" I ask, trying to keep my voice steady.

His eyes answer first, full of understanding. "Take all the time you need."

I turn and walk away, fast. Through my tears, I see Adam standing on the balcony. Instead of taking in the view, he's looking at me. He starts to approach, but I shake my head and walk past him, to the balcony railing, and I lean over the edge, feeling like I might vomit. Tears stream down my cheeks and out my nose. I gag, but nothing comes out.

"What's wrong?" Adam asks.

"I came all this way to find her," I say between sobs. "I *felt* her. This isn't how it was supposed to end." I suck in air desperately. My breaths are coming so fast that I feel like I'm going to pass out. I try to slow down my breathing, but I can't. My vision falters, turning black. "I can't … I can't."

Adam wraps his arms around me. It is the only thing that keeps me from losing it completely. I close my eyes, trying to focus.

"What happened over there?" Adam asks, holding me close to him. "What did he say?"

"She's dead." The words stab my ears. "My mom is dead."

But the man over at the café is my father. He is not the man I grew up thinking of as my father—that man was in my life, but never really in my life. Now I know that I have another father, a father who wasn't part of my life at all. A man who I don't know and who doesn't know me. But I think he *wants* to know me. I think he wants to be my father. When I looked into his eyes, I felt the way I used to feel in my mom's arms. Safe. This man being part of my life feels right. Like it is meant to be. Maybe fate brought me here today. To my father.

My body is shaking only slightly now, so lightly that it can't be seen, only felt. My breathing is slow and quiet "There's one more thing," I say to Adam, my voice calm and sure. "My father's alive."

* * *

Adam, my father, and I walk past bustling stalls selling souvenirs, toward tall torii gate with a huge, red paper lantern hanging below it.

"How long have you been in Japan?" my father asks me. It's the first thing he's said since we left the tourist information center.

"Just over a week," I say.

"Have you been outside of Tokyo?" he asks.

"We took day trips to Nikko and Kamakura. And we went to Kyoto, Nara, and Hakone." I reach into my backpack and take out my mom's bucket list. I unfold it. "We did everything on this list."

He touches the paper, as if it has awakened bittersweet memories. And then he smiles. "So did we."

I remember some of the moments in Japan where I thought I felt my mom's emotions: trepidation by the wish-granting water in Kyoto, panic inside the column behind the Buddha in Nara, excitement in Hakone near the torii gate on the lake. Maybe I was somehow experiencing memories of things that really happened.

"When she was collecting wish-granting water at Kiyomizu Temple, did she fall?" I ask.

"Nearly. She was reaching for a stream of water with the ladle. She wasn't very tall, so she had to lean forward quite a bit and she ..."

"... slipped." I don't phrase it as a question.

"How did you know—?"

"When she went through the tunnel in the column at Todaiji Temple, did she scream?" I can still hear the piercing cry that I heard when I was wedged inside that column.

"Oh yes." He nods vigorously. "Bloody murder."

"Did you go to the torii gate on Lake Ashi? It wasn't on her list, but—"

"She saw a photo of it on a poster at the train station, and we went on a quest to find it. We must have stood under that torii gate, looking out at the water, for over an hour. That's one of my happiest memories."

"I think it's one of her happiest memories too," I say.

"I think you're right," he says.

"This is going to sound crazy," I say, hoping that saying that will make what I'm about to say sound a little less foolish. "I felt like she was with me in those places."

"That doesn't sound crazy at all." He touches my shoulder lightly, awkwardly. "Sometimes I still feel like she's with me too."

"Do you know why my mom wanted to come to Japan?" I ask. It's a question I've had ever since my mom's friend gave me the bucket list almost one year ago. A question I thought only my mom would be able to answer.

He nods. "Her parents honeymooned here. They told your mom wonderful stories."

My mom's parents died in a car accident when she was a teenager. She must have missed them terribly. Like I miss her. Still, our losses were different. She knew her parents were dead. I was left to wonder.

"I want to show you something," my father says. He stops under the red lantern hanging from the torii gate. "Every day, many people walk under this lantern, but there's something only a small fraction of them ever do."

"What?" I ask.

"Look up," my father says.

Adam and I follow his gaze. Beneath the huge paper lantern—inside the golden circle of its base, where I would have expected to see nothing of interest—is an intricately-carved wooden picture of a dragon, accented with red paint.

We pose for some photos with the lantern and the gate: my father and me, and then Adam and me, and then all three of us. We pose for some silly photos too; the silly photos are my father's idea. I can't help feeling a little sad, imagining the dad that my father might have been to me, if he'd had the chance.

"When did my mom die?" I ask my father as we leave the gate.

"I don't know exactly."

"Weren't you ... with her?"

"We spent almost two weeks traveling around Japan, experiencing all the things she dreamed of doing. And then her health started to deteriorate. She was dying. She asked me to take her back to Tokyo to enroll in a clinical trial. She said that she wanted some good to come of her cancer; maybe others could be saved with the knowledge that the doctors gained by studying her. They put her on a drug regimen. And then something amazing happened: she got better. She started talking about going back home to New York. But then she took a turn for the worse. One morning, I woke up to a note."

"What did it say?" I ask.

"'Love, B.'"

"That's it?"

"That's it."

He wipes his moist eyes. I notice a wedding band on his left ring finger.

"Did you and my mom get married?" I ask.

"After your mom left, I waited many years. I felt like, by some miracle, I'd see her again. But eventually, I needed to try to move on. I married a wonderful woman who helped me deal with losing your mom. We have a son."

My pulse quickens with excitement. "I have a brother? Can I meet him?"

"How about tomorrow evening? We could all—"

"We leave tonight," I say.

He pulls out his phone. "Let me call my wife."

* * *

My father, Adam, and I take the train to Shinjuku. That's where my father lives. In the same neighborhood where Adam and I stayed on our few first days in Japan.

After we leave Shinjuku Station, we walk familiar streets that lead to vaguely-familiar streets. And then my father leads us down a narrow street that gives me an intense feeling of déjà vu. I look at the shops we pass, but I don't recognize any of them. Still, I feel like I've been here before.

Adam points ahead. "Erin, that's the restaurant where you saved that little kid."

My father turns to me. "You saved a kid?"

"A boy was choking," I explain. "I did the Heimlich Maneuver on him and CPR …"

My father's forehead furrows. "When did you do that?"

"On our first day in Japan," I say.

"Last Tuesday?" he asks.

"It was on the news?" I ask.

He shakes his head. "That boy was your brother."

* * *

A small boy opens the door to a tiny, two-story apartment in the same neighborhood where Adam and I wandered aimlessly eight days ago. "Daddy!" he exclaims, leaping into his father's arms, then he beams brightly at me. "Hi, I'm Koichi!"

He is definitely the same little boy from the restaurant.

I smile at him. "I'm Erin, and this is Adam."

"I remember you," he says, looking at me.

"I remember you too," I say softly.

But how, in a place as big as Japan, could I have found

both a father and a brother I never knew existed? It can't possibly be coincidence. I suppose it's possible that fate guided me to them. But I have a feeling that it was something—or rather some*one*—else. I think it was my mom. I think her spirit has been guiding me this whole trip.

A Japanese woman with dark hair that extends almost to her waist comes from inside the apartment. She gives Adam and me a small bow and then a smile. "I'm Hiroe," she says. "Welcome to our home. Please come in."

"Thank you," I say, stepping inside along with my father and Adam.

"What a beautiful yukata!" Hiroe says to me.

"Thank you." I slip off my shoes and place them beside the others.

As Hiroe and Adam introduce themselves, Koichi cocks his head to the side, studying me. "My mom told me you're my sister."

"Yes, I am," I say.

He looks at Adam. "Are you my brother?"

Adam smiles and shakes his head. "No."

Koichi shrugs awkwardly. "Want to see my trains?" he asks us.

"Of course," I say.

"Absolutely," Adam says.

Koichi jumps down from my father's arms, takes each of us by the hand, and hustles us past his mother, down the hallway, and into his bedroom. The room is crisscrossed with train tracks laid out in a circuitous route, passing through numerous makeshift tunnels.

Koichi lifts a small blue train that has a smiling face on the front. "This is Kikansha Tomasu. In America, his name is Thomas the Tank Engine," he says, and then he bursts into an explanation of Thomas' "special features." As he talks, a small cat with golden brown fur streaked in black—as if the cat slid through a chimney head-first— stalks into the room. Koichi takes a breath from his train monologue to say, "That's our cat. Her name is Hoshi." Then he slips right back into talking about trains without missing a beat.

Hoshi climbs into my lap and settles down. I stroke her back and she purrs loudly.

"Hoshi *likes* you!" Koichi says, sounding a bit surprised.

Hiroe pokes her head into the room. "Erin, Adam, we hope you'll stay for dinner."

"I'd really like that, but I ... I have kind of a special diet."

"It is the very least we can do," she says, looking at Koichi and then back at me. My father must have told her that I was the person who helped Koichi at the restaurant. "What type of diet do you have?"

"I'm allergic to shrimp. And I'm a vegetarian."

"As are your father and brother." She smiles. "You will join us then?"

I look at Adam, who nods. "We would love to," I say.

* * *

My father's dining room table is low, like the one at the okonomiyaki restaurant. My father, Hiroe, Adam, and I sit around the table on chairs that have backs but no legs. Koichi sits on a cushion with Hoshi in his lap.

"How old are you, Koichi?" Adam asks. I'm glad he asked because I keep forgetting to.

"Five years old," Koichi says, thrusting his shoulders back with pride.

"Do you go to school yet?" I ask.

"I go to Daddy's school," he says.

"I'm a teacher," my father explains.

"I thought you worked at the tourist center," I say.

"Your mom and I volunteered at the center after we moved to Tokyo," he says. "It was someplace she could go every day where she could help people. I still volunteer there about once a month … for her."

"Are the two of you in school?" Hiroe asks Adam and me.

"We go to college in New York," I say.

"New York!" Koichi says excitedly. "My daddy said we're going to go there someday on vacation. I want to climb up the stairs inside the Statue of Liberty and look out the windows in her hat." His eyes widen. "We can do it together! You, Adam, Mommy, Daddy, and me!"

I smile. "That sounds wonderful!"

When I was a kid, I spent a lot of time with my best friend and her family. I ate dinner at their house almost every night. I went with them to the park and the beach. Even on vacation a few times. But as much as they treated me like one of them, as much as I loved being with them, I constantly felt like an outsider. I always wished I had a family of my own. Where I felt I truly belonged. Maybe I had that once, but if I did, I can't remember what it was like.

I have a feeling that it feels like this.

* * *

My dad and Koichi accompany Adam and me back to our Shinjuku hotel to retrieve our luggage. Koichi bounces along by my side, holding my hand. I already love this little boy—my brother.

Adam and I collect our bags from the concierge, and then we stroll with our luggage toward the lobby. Suddenly, I see something that stops me dead in my tracks. Hanging on the wall is a framed sketch—so realistic that it looks like a photograph—of a traditional-looking Japanese bridge. I feel an instant surge of recognition even though I've never seen that bridge or this drawing before. There is a curvy signature in the corner. The same one that was on the sketch given to Adam by the old man. The sketch of the bridge in Nikko.

"That artist gave us one of his sketches," I say.

My dad moves closer to the wall, examining the sketch from an angle.

"What are you doing?" I ask.

"There's a hidden image in the picture." A moment later, he points at the trees to the right of the bridge. "There it is."

I take my dad's place, and I immediately see something I hadn't detected before. "A dog."

"Let me see!" Koichi says. Adam picks him up and they move to the side of the frame. Koichi points at the dog hidden in the trees. "I see him! I see him!"

"The dog is Hachikō," my dad says, referencing the informational plaque next to the sketch. "The artist puts hidden images in each of his sketches. He calls them 'the angels.'"

My hands shake as I lay my suitcase flat on the floor and pull out the oversized envelope where I placed the sketch that the old man gave to Adam to give to me. I slide the drawing out and examine it from different angles. Koichi joins me just as I see the turbulent water flowing over the rocks transform into the image of a woman. There is a necklace around the woman's neck with a small "B" in the center. I recognize the necklace and the woman from my most cherished photos.

Koichi leans close to the picture. "It's you," he says to me.

"No," I breathe. "It's my mom." I hand the sketch to my dad. "Did the artist know her?"

He holds the drawing at an angle, studying it, and then he inhales deeply. "Your mom took an art class in Nikko. She might have met him there." He hands the sketch back to me, and I carefully tuck it back into my suitcase.

"Maybe she went back to Nikko after she left Tokyo," I say. "Maybe that's where she …" My eyes burn. I don't want to cry in front of my little brother. "I'm going to go put on my travel clothes."

"We'll wait in the lobby," my dad says, taking Koichi's hand.

In the empty public restroom, tears spill down my cheeks as I remove my yukata and change into the same clothes I wore when I arrived in Japan. Once I've washed my face and combed my hair, I look fairly presentable.

Until I remember that I am about to do one of the hardest things I've done in my entire life: leave my family.

* * *

My dad insisted on wheeling my suitcase all the way from the hotel lobby to the train platform. As the train arrives, my dad pulls me close.

"Have a safe trip," he says. And then he whispers, "Adam seems like a great guy."

"He is," I whisper back.

Koichi pulls a Thomas the Tank Engine washcloth

from his pocket and rubs his wet eyes. "I wish you could stay," he says to me.

I give him a big hug. "I'll call you as soon as I get to New York," I assure him, holding back tears of my own.

Adam and I grab our suitcases and rush into the train just before the door closes. And then the train moves forward. My dad and Koichi wave at us and we wave back until we can't see them anymore. As soon as they are out of view, Adam and I fall into some seats. And I quietly fall apart.

* * *

A few minutes after we rise above the clouds over the Pacific Ocean, the flight attendant announces that it's safe to use approved electronic devices.

"Want to look at pictures from our trip?" Adam asks me, softly.

I smile for the first time in hours. "That would be nice."

Adam takes out his camera and holds it between us.

The first photo is of Adam and me at JFK airport in New York. Adam is pointing to the board at the gate where it says that the flight is going to Tokyo/Haneda. We're both wearing huge smiles—two best friends with no idea of what is about to happen. I feel like that photo was taken years rather than days ago. So much has changed between then and now.

The next picture is of me standing outside the Family Mart in Shinjuku, holding plastic bags filled with the items for our first breakfast in Tokyo. Then there are a few photos of the park where we ate. The Tokyo Metropolitan Government Office Building. My dad's neighborhood. The Hachikō statue. The neighborhood we passed through on our walk to Yoyogi Park. Meiji Jingu Shrine. The prayer plaques. A close-up of a prayer plaque … with Adam's handwriting on the plaque.

"You wrote a prayer?" I ask.

Adam inhales. "Yeah."

I squint at the picture. "What did you write?"

Adam hands me the camera. I zoom in on the photo and read the words neatly printed on the little wooden plaque: *I hope Erin finds what she is looking for.*

"I'm sorry it didn't work," Adam says.

I swallow against the lump in my throat. "Sometimes you don't know what you're looking for until you find it." I came to Japan to find my mom, and in a way, I *did* find her. And I found so much more. So much that I never knew I was missing.

When I came to Japan, I was lost.

I'm not lost anymore.

Six Months Later

My heart pounds and my breaths come fast. I never thought I'd spend Christmas Eve doing this.

"We're almost there!" a small voice says from behind me. Koichi's little hand slips into mine. He slides past me and drags me the rest of the way up the stairs. "This is so amazing!" he exclaims, looking up at the beam-filled interior of the Statue of Liberty's head. He pulls me to a window. "Can you lift me up, Erin?"

"I'll do it," my dad says. He grabs Koichi and lifts him so that he can see out the window.

"What do you see?" my dad asks. Strangely, his voice echoes inside my head.

I look down and see feet dangling in the air. My feet. They are toddler-sized and wear bright-pink sneakers decorated with cartoon kitty cats. I sense someone next to me. I turn my head to find ... my mom. She is about the same age as she is in the last photos I have of her, but she looks so much more beautiful than she does in any of those final photos. Because she is smiling. Big, strong, grownup hands are lifting me up to the crown window, but they aren't hers. I twist to see the face of the person holding me and recognize him instantly. He is the same man who stands next to me now, only he is many years younger.

"Dad?" I breathe.

"Yes?" my dad responds as Koichi wiggles down and goes over to touch one of the metal beams that arc up to the ceiling.

I shake off my daydream. Or was it a memory?

"I think I came here with my mom ..." I say, and then I add, "... and you."

"Your mom wanted to give you as many special moments with her as she could. The weekend before we left, she took you to some of her favorite places."

And suddenly, from his eyes, memories come flooding back to me. Listening to oars splash into the water in perfect rhythm as we glided in a rowboat across a lake in Central Park. Sitting in a soft, velvet seat watching a man and a woman in fancy costumes sing so powerfully that the walls of the ornate theater echoed their energy. Standing on a grassy lawn, staring upward, awed by the immense size of the Statue of Liberty. Things I did with my mom and the man who stands beside me now. He is in every one of those memories too.

"Why did *you* come with us?" I ask.

He inhales. "Your father was busy with work. Your mom was afraid to do it alone."

"I want to do all of those things again," I say. "With

you."

"That was my plan." He smiles and reaches into his pocket. "I suppose now is a good time to give you this." He places his hand over my mine and drops something small into my palm.

As soon as I see what it is, I feel an overwhelming ache in my chest. In my hand is tangible evidence that my mom is really gone: the "B" necklace she wore in every picture I've ever seen of her. I assume she never took it off.

"Where did you get this?" I ask him.

"She left it with her final note," my dad says. "I put it in my safe deposit box. I was going to bring it to you after you turned eighteen. I'd been planning to come this Christmas."

I wrap my fingers around the necklace. "You never would have found me. The bank sold my parents' house. I didn't leave a forwarding address. I wanted to start fresh …"

"Well then, it's a good thing *you* found *me*," he says.

Koichi runs up to us excitedly. "A lady said you can read the Statue of Liberty's book from over there!"

"Let's see!" my dad says.

As I follow my dad and Koichi, arms wrap around me from behind. I know they are Adam's. I spin around and embrace him.

"How's Hiroe?" I ask. Adam volunteered to stay with Hiroe when she needed a break on the long climb up the winding staircase to the top of the statue. Koichi tried to wait patiently, but he was practically bouncing with anticipation and so my dad, Koichi, and I went ahead.

"She's good," Adam says, gesturing to Hiroe, who is now looking out of a window, next to my dad and Koichi.

I hold out my hand and show him the necklace. "My dad gave it to me. It was my mom's."

"Do you want me to put it on you?" he asks.

I nod.

Adam carefully takes the necklace. I lift my hair and he joins his hands behind my neck. A moment later, the "B" rests on my chest, near my heart.

"Erin, Adam, we're over here!" Koichi calls out to us.

Koichi adores Adam. And the feeling is mutual. Adam is wonderful with children. Not only with Koichi. But also with his baby, Isamu.

We join my dad, Koichi, and Hiroe at the window. Adam slips behind me and puts his arms around me again. I take a deep, contented breath and look out into the distance. I focus on the spot where the world goes from clear to hazy.

And I smile.

About the author

J.W. Lynne has been an avid reader practically since birth and now writes inventive novels with twists, turns, and surprises. In the science fiction series THE SKY (ABOVE THE SKY, RETURN TO THE SKY, PART OF THE SKY, and BEYOND THE SKY), an eighteen-year-old fights to survive in a dystopian future society founded on lies. The romantic contemporary novels LOST IN LOS ANGELES and LOST IN TOKYO follow a young woman's journey after a horrible betrayal. KID DOCS dives into the behind-the-scenes action at a hospital where children are trained to become pint-sized doctors. In WILD ANIMAL SCHOOL, a teen spends an unforgettable summer working with elephants, tigers, bears, leopards, and lions at an exotic animal ranch.

Made in the USA
San Bernardino, CA
10 November 2019